**Praise for *It Starts with You***

"The guidebook parents need to end generational patterns, silence shame, and parent from a grace-based perspective."
—Kim Lange, MA, LCMHC, founder of Emotionanigans and Growing Up Confident

"A must-have resource for parents. . . . With a gentle, steady hand—never shaming, never blaming—Nicole Schwarz teaches what she calls parenting grace, a connection-based approach to calm, compassionate parenting."
—Dawn Huebner, PhD, author of *The Sibling Survival Guide* and *What to Do When You Worry Too Much*

"This heartfelt book is not about adding more to your parenting to-do list but rather about where to put your energy so that it truly counts. With great warmth and wisdom, this book weaves together personal stories, science, and practical tips."
—Ashley Söderlund, PhD, creator of Nurture and Thrive

"In her engaging and honest writing style, Nicole Schwarz helps parents get out of the shame spiral and focus on the power of grace when raising their children. The focus is on connection, not perfection, which is a breath of fresh air!"
—Janine Halloran, LMHC, founder of Coping Skills for Kids

# IT STARTS WITH YOU

## How Imperfect Parents Can Find Calm and Connection with Their Kids

**Nicole Schwarz, LMFT**

Broadleaf Books
Minneapolis

IT STARTS WITH YOU
How Imperfect Parents Can Find Calm and Connection with Their Kids

Cover design and illustration: Natalya Balnova

Print ISBN: 978-1-5064-7247-8
eBook ISBN: 978-1-5064-7248-5

*To my daughters*

# Contents

# Contents

# Foreword

Raising children is a beautiful, joyful, sometimes overwhelming and pressure-filled journey, and one that we all embark on with the highest of hopes and a good deal of preparation. Filled to the brim with nearly equal amounts of love and anxiety, we read, research, and nest our way through months of anticipation, only to learn that nothing at all could have truly prepared us for parenthood. Each child comes to us with a unique soul, and there are no how-to books or manuals for how to guide that particular, unique child to adulthood successfully. How could there be? This child has never existed before.

In truth, if your child had come with a manual, it would have likely been a disservice to you because it would have kept you stuck on a predestined path with no curiosity or room to grow. When we get right down to it, so much of our parenting journey is about growth—not just the child's but, importantly, our own as well. Parenthood is the sacred ground where we get to rise to our own potential. On this journey, we are able to examine ourselves and our stories, trim away the beliefs and habits which do not serve us, and come out the other side wholly changed. To do that, we will need to hold hands with others who inspire and teach us along the way.

This is how I first came across the compassionate wisdom of Nicole Schwarz. She has been a guiding light for parents for many years, and I was drawn to not only her practical positive parenting advice, but her gentle and inspiring tone. Schwarz understands that there is no magic trick for how to raise children but that connection, empathy, and heaping doses of compassion are the keys to a happier parenting journey. All change begins within. In *It Starts with You*, she has beautifully woven this practical advice together with her inspirational voice and abundant compassion to bring you a book that feels like a warm embrace from a beloved friend.

In the opening chapters, you will quickly see that this is not a parenting book that demands perfection in its techniques or that promises lofty results. Rather, Schwarz gently encourages you to do the self-work necessary to show up at your best for your child. Early on in the very first chapter, she takes your hand and comes alongside you to discuss important topics that weigh heavily on the hearts of parents like shame and imperfection. She shows you how to adopt a grace-based mindset, to see mistakes as part of the learning process, and how to parent from a healthier, more realistic perspective.

Self-work is some of the most important work of parenthood. Until we understand our strengths and weaknesses, our origins of beliefs, and our own feelings and behaviors, it is difficult to show up with grace and intention. So, in chapters two and three, you will begin the process of self-reflection, owning your own behavior, and taking responsibility for your story. Knowing yourself and why you respond the way you do will help you be a better parent, and Schwarz helps you explore your parenting story and rewrite old narratives that currently limit you. Most parents pick up parenting books to help fix their child's behavior not realizing that their own behavior often needs fixing first. It can be uncomfortable work, but Schwarz lovingly guides you through it with her professional knowledge and personal empathy.

Understanding and managing emotions is work we all want our children to do, but to teach them how to do this effectively, we must become good at it ourselves. The following two chapters will help you explore your emotions. Schwarz walks you through exploring your feelings and how to playfully explore them with your kids. It's okay to feel all of your emotions and to allow your child to feel them, too. Your child doesn't need a robot parent, but someone who models emotional regulation. She shows you how to do just that while understanding that no parent is going to do it perfectly every time, and so you'll learn what to do when you make a mistake to repair the relationship and reestablish connection.

Many times, a child's behavior is not a result of ill will but of immaturity. In my own work, I've seen how understanding your child's brain development greatly improves empathy and understanding. Chapters 6 through 10 teach you must-know information about the functions of the brain. Don't worry if this sounds overwhelming. You don't need to be a neuroscientist to be a good parent! Understanding your child's behavior and your own responses starts with understanding the basics of how the brain works, and Schwarz provides simple and easy to understand information about how the brain functions. You'll learn how to identify stressors and how to manage your stress response, and in turn, you'll know how to help your child do the same.

Because healthy brains need healthy connections, this book will teach you how to use calmness and connection to help your child's brain "wire together" optimally. Schwarz shows you how to make real life connections to consistently remind your kids that they belong. You'll learn how to figure out what makes each of your children feel love and connected, and armed with this knowledge, you'll see your relationships flourish.

Schwarz will show you how to break your child free from The Bad Kid Cycle, how to combat shame and change your story about your worth, how to connect better, listen well, and have healthy communication skills with your family, and how to use empathy to strengthen your relationships in chapters 13 through 18. These are all powerful remedies to disconnection and unwanted behavior which I've seen work time and again to transform the lives and relationships of families.

Throughout the rest of the book, Schwarz teaches you crucial problem-solving skills, factors that impact behavior, and how to challenge your current beliefs about discipline and begin to parent without punishment. She shows you how to give your children the amazing gift of unconditional love as you come alongside your child through every stage to teach and guide from a place of love, trust, and relationship.

*It Starts with You* is ultimately a book about being. Being attuned. Being present. Being intentional. Being creative. Being confident. You will be lovingly guided through a transformation as you read this book, and that is Schwarz' gift to all of the parents that are lucky enough to be touched by her work. No longer bound by perfection or restricting parenting "shoulds," you will reap the lasting benefits of a connected relationship with your children and the knowledge to guide them through every age and stage with confidence and love. Let the journey to grace-based parenting begin.

Rebecca Eanes
Author of *Positive Parenting: An Essential Guide*

# Introduction

**When I brought my oldest daughter** home from the hospital in 2008, I was under the impression there was a "right" way to parent her. If only I could get her to sleep, eat, poop, and cry on a schedule, she would turn out all right. It didn't take long for this tiny baby to show me that she was not going to fit into any neat and tidy boxes. She had a strong personality, cried often, and was difficult to soothe. I felt stuck. I thought, *What do I do now?*

Parenting books at the time were filled with suggestions and "how-tos," all focused on her behavior and things I could do to make her fit the mold of a "good child."

There was nothing about me or my behavior.

What I didn't know then was she had undiagnosed celiac disease and was most likely in pain after every feeding. What I didn't know then was that she would need extra help soothing her nervous system to feel calm. And maybe most importantly, what I didn't know then was how my anxiety about parenting her "correctly" got in the way of parenting her well.

I've grown a lot since those overwhelming newborn days. We've added two more daughters to our family. I've shifted my professional focus from providing mental health therapy to children to supporting parents as a coach. I've immersed myself in research about brain development, shame, and the power of relationships.

And though I have not fully arrived, I'm learning to embrace imperfection. Recognizing I am never going to be perfect—and reminding myself that my kids do not need me to be perfect.

They need me to be present.

This is not a "how-to" parent book. This is not a book with all the answers to all your parenting dilemmas.

This is a book about having a grace-filled mindset. A perspective that prioritizes relationships over rules. Connection over consequences. How to "be" rather than what to "do."

Each chapter in this book is written with the intention of helping you grow in your ability to teach and guide your kids with calm confidence. No more parenting from a place of panic, worry, pressure, or desperation. No more doing things one way because that's how you were raised. No more crossing your fingers and hoping things will just go away on their own.

There is a plan here, but we need to start at the beginning. And the beginning—is you.

I encourage you to read the book from start to finish rather than jumping around. Each section builds on the one before. I believe effective parenting starts with knowing ourselves, recognizing areas of growth, and celebrating progress (even if it seems small). Then we need to learn how to calm our brains so we can make confident parenting decisions. Next, we need to connect with our kids so they feel secure—seen, known, and loved. After that, we may need to make a few changes to the way we communicate with our kids or take time to identify assumptions that impact our reactions and responses. And finally, we need to think about discipline as teaching and guiding. Recognizing maturity and brain development cannot be rushed; we need to accept all emotions—even the big, uncomfortable ones—and learn how to have respectful disagreements with those we love the most.

Grace-filled parenting takes patience and time. It takes energy and insight. In some cases, it means making brave changes to the way you're doing life right now.

But this is not about doing more. Instead of doing a complete parenting overhaul, the goal is to help you put your energy into the things that need your attention the most right now while letting other things go. Being intentional about your parenting decisions helps you grow more fully into the calm, confident, connected caregiver your children desperately need: never growing perfectly, just taking one step at a time, making steady progress in a positive direction.

As you weave your way through these pages and dig into new parenting strategies, you may feel emotions stirring inside. You may recognize fears, worries, stress, or trauma you didn't even know you were carrying. You may feel a sense of loneliness or uncertainty. Regardless of your response, please know that you do not need to muscle through each day alone. Sometimes we need more than a close friend, spouse, or colleague to get us through. Mental health providers are trained to support you through these discoveries and see you through to the other side. Seeking support does not mean you are flawed, broken, or damaged but that you are willing to take the steps needed to be the healthiest version of yourself possible. There are challenges to seeking support—finding a babysitter, making the payments, finding someone you trust, receiving criticism from relatives—but none of these are more important than your well-being. If you read something in this book that triggers you, challenges you, or shines a light on a difficult area of your life or your child's life, please reach out to a professional.

Holding a mirror up to examine ourselves can be uncomfortable. The tendency is to point out our flaws, demonstrate the numerous ways we fall short, and explain, in detail, how we've failed our kids or our families over the years. It's so much easier to be critical than compassionate.

The questions and suggestions in this book are meant to help you grow and flourish in your parenting. Noticing an area where you'd like to improve does not mean you've failed. It means you can now see a clear path in the direction you'd like to head. Becoming aware of a habit doesn't mean there's something wrong with you; it means you're in a better position to form a new pattern.

But the only way this is going to work is if we treat ourselves with kindness. Forgiving what needs forgiving, taking responsibility without adding unnecessary guilt, and recognizing that our past—while important—does not dictate our future. You are here now. You are willing to explore, think critically, and maybe even try something new. That is exciting!

Let this be a process.

You are not alone; I'm right there with you. I am constantly growing, learning, and adapting as I raise my daughters. We work through the ups and downs of sibling relationships, social conflicts, emotions, communication, anger, anxiety, and everything else that comes with being in a family. Sometimes things work together beautifully. We laugh, hug, and enjoy each other's company. Sometimes we argue, cry, and escape to separate corners of the house.

This is life in an imperfect family.

You have your own beautifully unique, imperfect family. Our celebrations and conflicts may look different, but in the

end, none of us truly have this parenting thing "all figured out."
Some days will be amazing. Some days will be difficult. Rather
than trying to rush maturity or expect overnight success, let's
take a deep breath.

We'll get there. One step at a time.

Moving forward in a positive direction, embracing the
not knowing, and welcoming imperfections with grace and
compassion.

It starts with you, so let's get started.

# CHAPTER 1

# Parenting without Shame

**I wave as the bus drives** away. I force a smile across my tear-stained face.

My daughter's face is plastered to the bus window. She looks like she's close to tears too.

I fight an urge to run after the bus, flag it down, and pull her into one last tight hug.

Our morning was rough. Actually, most school mornings are rough. My daughter despises the mundane tasks of lunch-packing, doing homework, and finding clean socks. The routine cramps her creativity and fly-by-the-seat-of-her-pants personality. And so each morning, I brace myself for what's to come.

Though the clock says she has twenty minutes until the bus arrives, the panic inside her builds. She feels rushed and stressed. This inner turmoil soon boils outward; she's snapping at her sisters, demanding help with breakfast, and exploding at a minor misunderstanding.

Some days I can stay calm and supportive. I know she's just feeling overwhelmed. And I'm able to resist responding back with the same tone she's using with me.

But today I am tired. I know she is having a hard time, but my own exhaustion catches up with me. "It's not a big deal!" I say, exasperated. "Whatever socks you can find are fine! Just get moving!"

Those words hit her like a ton of bricks. It *is* a big deal to her. And instead of motivating her, telling her to hurry up causes her to slam on the brakes.

"I'm not going!" she yells back, digging in her heels.

"Yes, you are. Come on. It's OK. You'll make it to the bus on time . . ." My voice wavers between gentle and about to lose my cool.

Somehow we make it to the bus stop. I do my best to be cheerful: "Look for the positive! It's a beautiful day!" But I know these platitudes only minimize the complicated feelings she has inside.

I fold her into a tight bear hug as the bus approaches.

On days like these, my inner parenting voice whispers, "You shouldn't have rushed to get her on the bus today. She needed you. She was obviously upset."

Initially, I brush it aside. Clearly this morning was not a complete failure, right? She got on the bus, we ended on good terms, and I didn't yell at the top of my lungs. But the voice is persistent: "You should have . . ." or "You shouldn't have . . ." or "How could you . . . ?"

And the spiral begins: "I shouldn't have put her on the bus. I wasn't in tune with her emotions. She needed me. I let her down."

"I did the best I could" becomes "I am a failure."

"I made a mistake" becomes "I am a mistake."

In an instant, a normal parenting challenge leaves me feeling completely flawed. Guilt turns to shame.

## EMBRACING IMPERFECTION

On the surface, we all know perfection is impossible to achieve. When our toddlers fall while learning to walk, we say, "Oops! Up you go. Try again!"

But when it comes to parenting—our parenting—the story we tell ourselves is a bit different.

This story tends to be an all-or-nothing endeavor. It carries an unspoken expectation of perfection. We measure ourselves by our behavior and by the behavior of our children. If you lose your cool instead of staying calm just once, it wipes out all those other times you were able to stay calm in the heat of the moment. If your child melts down at the end of a playdate, you feel a nagging tug as if something you did (or failed to do) caused it.

Rather than seeing these moments as learning opportunities or normal developmental stages, we keep lists of our mistakes. In quiet moments, this "evidence" seems to pile up against us. Times we should have comforted when instead we punished. Situations where we unfairly judged the circumstances without knowing the facts. Places we missed opportunities to show love and criticized instead. It's easy to see how shame can take hold. Over time, we start believing the lie that says, "I'm a failure."

*Healthy* guilt enables us to take responsibility, admit our flaws, and move forward. "I'm sorry I lost my cool with you. It was wrong of me to overreact like that." Hugs all around, and everyone moves forward in a positive direction.

*Unhealthy* guilt moves quickly to shame. Shame is the desire to hide true feelings for fear that you will be unlovable. Shame researcher Brené Brown defines shame as "the intensely painful feeling or experience of believing that we are flawed and therefore unworthy of love and belonging—something we've experienced, done, or failed to do makes us unworthy of connection."[1] While guilt says, "I made a mistake," shame says, "I *am* a mistake."

Confident parenting requires a willingness to look at our own behavior. It insists that we honestly take stock of our thoughts, words, and actions. It assumes that you have the desire to use guilt in a healthy way and push through those lonely, isolating, uncomfortable feelings of shame to make changes.

This is not easy.

If you've never named that little voice in your head that makes you doubt if you're a "good enough" parent, welcome to shame. If you've been stuck in a shame spiral for years, you may worry that there's no way out. It's true that shame is a powerful force and that it takes work to silence those dishonest messages. But committing to breaking the cycle of shame is one of the best gifts we can give our children. It starts with you. Deciding today that you will no longer define yourself, your parenting, or your worth through the lens of shame—as a failure or a mistake. Instead, embracing the fact that you are worthy of love simply because you're you.

Shame wants to keep you stuck, hidden, disconnected from a community. But here's the truth: your kids don't need perfect parents. You don't have to create the perfect solution, say the exact right thing, or maintain complete neutrality in every argument. In fact, messy, busy, forgetful, angry, anxious, impulsive kids can find a lot of comfort in knowing they are not the only ones who have things to learn.

When your kids see you embracing imperfection and refusing to be paralyzed by shame, you give them permission to see mistakes as part of the growing up process rather than something that needs to be hidden, pushed down, or perfected in order to be loved. In other words, you keep them from becoming entangled in their own shame spiral.

## GRACE-BASED PARENTING

This book is a guide, a logical progression of strategies to help you make parenting choices with confidence. However, this is not a test of your perfection. It's not a "do this and have perfect kids" guarantee either.

You can follow the advice in this book and still occasionally yell at your kids. You can use these tips and your kids may still have an argument with each other or refuse to turn off the TV. Not many parenting books start with this kind of statement. But I'm being honest. And if we admit that perfection is impossible, this honesty is where we need to start.

The fact that you make a mistake doesn't necessarily mean you're doing something wrong. Or that the information in this book doesn't work. Or that YOU are a mistake. It means you're imperfect. And so are your kids. Sure, there are things we can improve on, which is why you're reading this, I assume. But we don't want to fall prey to the extreme view that the only way we measure success is by never showing a big emotion again or avoiding conflict at all costs.

Parenting from a healthier, more realistic perspective is a commitment. It's an opportunity for you to say, "I'm not going to have this all figured out right away, and that's OK. In fact, I'm never going to do this 100 percent perfectly, and that's OK too.

I can learn from my mistakes and move forward in a positive direction."

I call this grace-based parenting.

"Grace" means being abundantly generous with yourself and others. Recognizing we all struggle and make mistakes. That love doesn't require perfection. Being quick to take responsibility for our part, focusing on connection rather than being "right," working to repair the relationship and forgive.

Of course, some may say this mindset ignores wrongdoing. Or that it's too permissive or minimizes sinful behavior.

In my faith background, there was a lot of focus on sin. We were encouraged to meditate on the things we did wrong, the ways we hurt others, and how we disrupted the relationship between ourselves and God. I was great at listing my failures. I knew exactly what I had done wrong. In fact, I could write a detailed list for you on the spot. On the outside, I was a "good kid." On the inside, I thought of myself as a mistake, as the culmination of all my "failures." Instead of turning me toward repentance, it dug me deeper into shame.

Now looking back, I realize that by focusing so much on my sin, I missed the concept of grace. The knowledge that I am loved and cherished in my messiness. That it is not my consistent imperfection that nailed Jesus to the cross, but his love for me in spite of this imperfection. It's through this love that I can take an honest look at my sin and repent rather than admitting it out of shame. Your faith upbringing may have been very different—if you grew up with faith at all. Regardless, most of us picked up an unhealthy focus on our faults when what we really need as parents is grace—for ourselves and for our kids.

A quote from parenting expert Pam Leo is making the rounds on social media. It says, "We can't teach children to behave better by making them feel worse."[2] We cannot start by pointing out our children's flaws and imperfections and expect them to make a healthy change in behavior. We need to start with connection. We need to start with love. We need to be willing to give them grace first—even before they change their behaviors.

Your kids are going to make mistakes. They are going to test the limits and engage in power struggles. They are going to act out when their brain is in panic mode. Grace-based parenting doesn't mean we can't hold a boundary or set a limit. It's not one or the other; it's both. It's grace and love *and* boundaries and safety.

When we start with grace, we say, "You are valuable to me. The relationship I have with you is more important than being right or having the last word." We build a bridge. We set a foundation of trust. Our kids begin to learn that it's safe to be honest, it's safe to apologize, and it's safe to make mistakes because our love isn't based on their perfection.

Grace-based parenting doesn't mean glossing over things to only focus on the good; rather, it's to give ourselves a clear picture. A picture defined by truth, not by shame. When we lose our tempers, we recognize the voice in our head that whispers, "Failure. Failure. How could you do that again?!" And we challenge it and gently rephrase it as "OK. That got offtrack quickly. I am feeling overwhelmed by my child's big feelings. That's a normal response in this situation. What do I need to do to get back to feeling calm so I can make this right with him?"

You are imperfect. So are your kids. This book will help you embrace imperfection and cling to grace so you can shed the weight of shame and parent your kids with confidence.

# IT STARTS WITH YOU

- How do you define *shame* and *guilt*?

- How would you define *grace-based parenting*?

- In what areas of your parenting do you find yourself struggling to embrace imperfection?

- What shame-based messages do you tell yourself?

# CHAPTER 2

# It Starts with You

**Years ago, when I was just** starting out as a therapist, I got a job doing in-home family therapy. My clients were children who struggled to manage their anger, anxiety, ADHD, or aggression. The goal was to bring the family together to talk about the child's challenging behavior and find a way to make it decrease. Using the popular intervention tools of the time, we created endless charts. Rules, consequences, rewards. Points, tokens, stickers. Elaborate schemes to encourage the child to behave in a way the family deemed "acceptable."

In all my years sitting with families, the focus was always on the child. Hoping we could motivate them to do better, speak kinder, or manage their emotions. I can't recall a time when I created a chart to help the parents to manage their own emotions. The general (though unspoken) message was clear: "I'm fine. Fix my kid."

You'll notice that there aren't any lists of rewards and consequences in this book. There are no instructions for making an effective point system. After stumbling across positive parenting in my research, I quickly abandoned the notion that our immature children should somehow have the skills, knowledge, and ability to manage their behavior better than the adults providing their care simply because they earned a sticker.

And before you think I'm pointing the finger here, please know that I include myself in the "fix my kid" category. I will be the first to admit that it is much easier to expect someone else to do the difficult work of changing their behavior than to look at my own—even if that other person is a child. Though it's easier now than it was at the beginning, I still slip into this mindset, especially when I'm tired, stressed, or overwhelmed.

## AN EXHAUSTING CYCLE

No one wakes up in the morning thinking, "I hope I yell at my kids today!" No one hopes they'll get so angry, they take away their children's privileges. And yet, we find ourselves in these positions time and time again.

Often this cycle starts when we are in the "fix my kid" mentality. The thinking goes like this: you talk about acceptable behavior, set up rewards for achieving this behavior, and give consequences for negative behavior. Sometimes these rewards work! Your child follows through with the behavior you were hoping to see, and everyone's happy. Unfortunately, more than likely, your child doesn't achieve this behavior—so you dole out consequences. This, as you probably know from experience, doesn't go well. Your child begs and pleads. They promise things will be different. They tell you they didn't mean it. All the parenting books you read told you to be consistent, to stick to what you say you're going to do, and so you keep the consequence in place.

But then something happens: your child doesn't relent. They persist. They get more upset. They yell and scream. They call you names. Your own temper rises, and you find yourself feeling even angrier. Feeling trapped, you increase the consequences.

Raise the stakes. Which, of course, makes everything worse. Your child is even more upset. And now you are yelling. Pulling your child forcefully into their room until *they* calm down.

Later, when the dust settles, the conversation centers once again on the child's behavior. Lectures begin with, "If you would have emptied the dishwasher when I asked, you wouldn't have lost your screen time." Or, "If you would have left the park without a tantrum, Mommy wouldn't have yelled."

Cue shame. That little voice inside whispering, "Good moms don't yell at their kids." Or, "Good parents raise children who listen the first time." And you make a pact with yourself: tomorrow I'm not going to yell.

It's an exhausting cycle. Maybe you can relate.

The goal of this book is to break this cycle. To give you another option. We'll talk about your kids' response in these difficult situations in a later section. But first, we need to talk about you.

## THE MOST IMPORTANT FIRST STEP

It seems easier to put the focus on our kids; getting them to change their behavior would make parenting so much easier! But grace-based parenting is about us first, not our children. It's about owning our part in the drama, being honest with ourselves about our challenges and struggles, and doing the work needed to be the mature one in the relationship.

This is not easy.

How many times do we tell our kids to stop doing something because it is inconvenient or annoying? How often do we want our kids to stop acting like children and start acting more like us? How often do we desire our toddlers to ask for attention with words they don't have? Or expect our older kids to stay quiet in the precoffee morning hours instead of energetically soaking up the amazing new day before them?

For many of us, this is a daily practice.

Remember the previous scenario? Remember how you felt in that situation? I don't want you to feel stuck, parenting from a place of frustration or anger. I want you to find the freedom to parent with calm confidence. And there's only one way I know to find that peace; it's by working on yourself first.

## CHANGING THE QUESTION

In the sea of parenting advice swirling around the internet, the majority of posts focus on "How to get your child to . . . (fill in the blank with desired behavior)." While this advice may be helpful, my guess is very few of these articles include space for you to explore your own thoughts, habits, words, and actions that impact your child's behavior. You can try a million different strategies and find yourself stuck in the same place. To move forward in a positive direction, we need to start by shifting from a "fix my kid" mindset to an "it starts with me" mindset.

Here are some examples:

- Before you ask, "How do I get him to listen?" I'd encourage you to ask, "How can I speak in a way that encourages listening?"

- Before you ask, "How do I get her to brush her teeth without complaining?" I'd encourage you to ask, "Why does her resistance bother me so much?"

- Before you ask, "Why won't he calm down?" I'd encourage you to ask, "How can I keep myself calm, even when he is upset?"

Notice the focus is on the parent—our actions, our behaviors, our triggers—rather than the child. We're saying, "I know I'm part of this problem. What changes can I make that may move this forward in a positive, respectful way?" We're not waiting for our children to get their act together first. We're not pointing the finger. We're not making assumptions about our children's motivation or expecting them to suddenly act like mature adults. We're recognizing that we have some work to do so we can be calm, confident guides for our children.

Changing the question may require you to adopt a totally new way of thinking. You may not be used to exploring your thoughts, feelings, or behaviors. You may have no idea how to shift the focus from your child to yourself without piling on the guilt (or heading down a shame spiral). Our busy lives and endless to-do lists do not leave much room for self-reflection. It's OK if this feels confusing or uncomfortable at first. The process of self-reflection will be different for everyone. Some parents choose to write their answers in a journal or talk it through with a coparent or close friend. Some parents find that they cannot rephrase questions or explore the answers without the help of a mental health professional. An outside perspective can be helpful, spotlighting things we overlook, noticing ingrained patterns, and gently guiding us toward health.

This is not the last time we will talk about noticing and being aware of our thoughts and feelings—this theme runs through the entire book. The tips and strategy discussed all assume the "it starts with you" mindset, giving you plenty of opportunities to practice noticing, shifting the focus, and parenting in a calm, confident way.

The goal here is to own our story—our reactions, our behaviors, our words—rather than shifting the responsibility to our children. We're the ones with mature, developed brains. We're the ones with life experience. And we're the ones who set the tone for our families. When we look at ourselves first, we can model and guide our kids in a way that helps them learn, grow, and embrace these skills as their own. Welcoming imperfection and giving plenty of grace along the way.

So before we get to the "how-tos," let's start with you. And me. The adult. The parent. And let's agree to give ourselves plenty of grace as we pick apart the pieces we bring to this relationship.

## IT STARTS WITH YOU

- How does it feel to have to wait to get to the "how-tos"?

- What parts of parenting right now don't fit with the parent you want to be?

- Are you willing to look at yourself first? Why or why not?

# CHAPTER 3

# Owning Your Story

**My youngest daughter is an extrovert;** being with people makes her feel energized. She's also a talker. From a very early age, she was narrating even the smallest details of our daily routine. This is not just small talk or nonsense-babble; she's looking for a conversation. The listener needs to be present, attentive, and responsive.

When her sisters are busy or my husband is at work, she has an audience of one: me. Unfortunately, I am an introvert. I am energized by having time alone, quiet, and space to think. I don't speak up in groups unless I truly have something important to say. I can be outgoing, silly, and chatty with my close friends and family, but even those moments wear on me over time.

After a day together, my daughter will feel content and connected while I feel drained and exhausted. This is not a criticism of my daughter; I love spending time with her, listening to her stories, questions, and observations. This is about my temperament, my personality, how I'm wired. I simply feel drained after that much conversation, no matter who's doing the talking!

Knowing this about myself helps me be a better parent.

But it hasn't always been this way.

For most of my life, the word *introvert* wasn't in my vocabulary. All I knew was that after spending a long day with my kids where I was required to do a lot of listening, talking, or interacting, my body felt tense, my temper was short, clutter bothered me, and I was quick to notice the negative. All I wanted was some time alone, but asking for a break felt selfish. Unspoken thoughts swirled through my mind: "Good moms enjoy spending time with their kids," and "Good moms don't need breaks." So I snapped at my kids, felt bad about it, and hoped everyone would eventually give me the space I was craving.

Embracing my introverted nature is one of the many lessons I've learned about myself over the years. Shifting the focus from my kids' behavior to my own forced me to acknowledge the intricacies that make me who I am and helped me learn more about why I react the way I do in certain situations. It took some time to recognize when I needed a break. It took even more time to realize that taking a break doesn't make me a "bad mom." Reading a few chapters of a book by myself or plugging in my earbuds (a clear sign that mom is "talked out") isn't selfish or abnormal. It means I'm an introvert! Filling this need gives me the energy to connect with my kids in the way that works best for them. Which, for my youngest, will always be having a conversation.

Your life experience, your family upbringing, your environment, your work life, your support system, your nervous system, and your personality all impact your parenting. When we ignore or minimize these experiences, we ignore a huge part of our parenting story. Author Aundi Kolber explains it this way: "When we deny the reality of our experiences, we don't become more of who God designed us to be, but less. There's no way to have cohesive stories unless we truly embrace all it: the good, the hard, the bittersweet, the sad, the joyful, the lonely, and the painful. It all counts."[1]

The reason you yell at your kids might be because it was modeled by your own parents, who handled conflict by screaming. It might be because you feel out of control. It might be because your nervous system is overstimulated. Chances are it's a combination of many things. None of these things make you a bad or worthless parent. But some of these things impact your parenting in a negative way. Yelling at your kids may make you feel less like the parent you want to be and more like a parent you recognize from your childhood—or one you barely recognize at all.

Starting with you means being willing to explore, tell, and embrace your story. The good, the bad, and the ugly. You cannot recognize what needs to be changed until you take the time, space, and patience to explore it. It's not easy, but it is an important step to moving forward in a positive direction.

This may be an unusual place to start a parenting book. Most parents read books to find answers. To-do lists. Strategies. Tips. But if we're not careful, these answers will come from a "fix my kid" mentality. I want you to feel equipped to parent with confidence. I want you to be empowered, knowing what to do, not because a book tells you, but because you are able to calmly assess the situation. Your kids feel connected to you, you communicate with respect, and you focus on teaching, rather than punishment. The goal is to strive not for perfect parenting but parenting filled with grace and kindness for yourself and your kids.

To do this, you need to own your story.

## NOTICING AND NAMING YOUR STORY

Imagine your story like a messy junk drawer. The problem with messy junk drawers is that it's difficult to find the things you need. You may be looking for a screwdriver but have to dig under the stapler, stamps, and batteries to find it. It's the same with our messy parenting junk drawer. It's full of life experiences, thoughts, triggers, emotions, reactions, and beliefs we bring to our parenting relationships. It's all important, but most of it is jumbled, ignored, or minimized because either we avoid the story or we haven't spent much time exploring it.

Organizing the kitchen junk drawer makes it easier to find the things we need. Noticing, naming, and embracing your parenting junk drawer allows you to create a narrative that guides your parenting in a positive direction rather than keeping you stuck in old patterns, habits, and routines.

If you want to know why you're so prone to hiding in your closet when your kids have a meltdown, you may need to dig through your childhood, learn about your temperament, and understand what your brain does under stress. Acknowledging this information gives you the opportunity to change the story you tell yourself. Instead of "I'm a failure because I can't stay in the room when my kids are crying," your story can be "My brain goes into flight mode when I'm stressed, and I'm learning ways to calm my brain so I can stay present with my kids when they're upset."

Noticing and naming experiences, thoughts, and beliefs may not come naturally at first. You may feel some resistance, confusion, or even an urge to move on to a different chapter. That is normal. Maybe today you just skim through, deciding to go back and dig in with more detail later. Exploring our parenting junk drawer may take months or even years. The more often you notice and name things, the more opportunities you have to create a positive narrative. And the more often you practice, the easier it will be to recognize when old habits pop up or when something from your past is impacting your behavior.

Some stories are layered with too much pain, hurt, sadness, or anger to look at on our own. Opening these stories without the support of a mental health professional would be unsafe or unhealthy. If you feel stuck, overwhelmed, ashamed, defensive, avoidant, or angry about a part of your parenting story, make an appointment with a mental health professional and work through it together. Seeking support is not a sign of weakness; it demonstrates that you are working to be the healthiest version of yourself for your children.

## YOUR PARENTING STORY

Pause and think about your parenting story, or use a few of the prompts that follow to help you explore and name things that impact your parenting. You may decide to journal your responses, make notes about something you want to explore in more depth, or compare notes with a coparent, friend, or mental health professional.

The goal isn't to create a "perfect" narrative. Be honest with yourself. Even if that means admitting something embarrassing, difficult, or imperfect. Work hard not to judge your reactions or responses. Remember, we're dumping the junk drawer out on the counter, picking things apart, putting things in categories, organizing—just noticing. Rather than saying, "What is wrong with me?" just notice: "I know I need a lot of sleep, and I haven't been sleeping well lately. I dread dropping my daughter off at daycare because I know she'll cry, and I feel embarrassed leaving her like that. Evenings are stressful because I believe a good mom makes homemade meals, and honestly, I'm not a great cook. It's no wonder I'm feeling overwhelmed."

There is no "good" or "bad" here, only information. Remember: be kind and gracious to yourself.

## EXPERIENCES, THOUGHTS, AND BELIEFS

Use the following questions as a guide to help you explore your parenting story. Some questions may be simple to answer, while others may require more processing, writing, or talking to others to clarify your thoughts. If you are coparenting, you may decide to discuss the questions together, becoming aware of the stories each of you brings to the parenting experience.

Start by exploring your own childhood.

- How was discipline handled in your family?

- Who did most of the caretaking?

- How would you describe the communication, especially around conflict?

- What emotions were acceptable and which ones were ignored, minimized, or dismissed?

- Who made you feel the most loved?

- What did they do (or not do) that made you feel that closeness?

- What traits, phrases, or behaviors do you display that are similar to your caregivers' growing up?

- In what ways are you different?

Now think about what makes you unique as a person.

- When do you feel most energized?

- What makes you feel drained?

- How would you describe your temperament?

- What are your strongest skills and talents?

- What are some areas you'd like to grow in?

- Is it difficult or easy to show grace and kindness to yourself?

- What needs do you have that are not being met?

Next, think about your journey to parenthood.

- Was it a delightful experience?

- Was it full of disappointment, discouragement, sadness, or pain?

- How did this experience compare with your expectations of becoming a parent?

- How do you define a "good" parent?

Explore your current stage of life.

- What do you expect from your kids at this stage?

- What makes this stage difficult?

- How is this stage better than the one you just left?

- What parts of parenting feel like a burden right now?

- What parts are bringing you joy?

How do you feel about your kids?

- Are you feeling close, or is the relationship strained? (Maybe some days are better than others.)

- What do you love about your child?

- Which behaviors cause you the most concern?

- Are you feeling exhausted by a particular behavior or a current challenge?

- How are you and your child alike?

- How are you different?

- How does this affect the way you interact with each other?

- Which behaviors remind you of yourself as a child?

- Which behaviors would have been unacceptable in your home?

Think about the expectations you have for yourself or your kids.

- Are these expectations reasonable?

- Are they age-appropriate?

- Where did these expectations come from?

- Are they handed down generationally?

- Are they defined by your own sense of shame or embarrassment?

- Are they being explicitly stated by someone?

- Which of these expectations would you like to let go?

Finally, think about your sensory threshold. Some people are more sensitive to smells, sounds, textures, activity levels, and environmental stimulation, like the lighting in a room.

- Which sensory experiences cause you to feel calm and peaceful?

- Which ones cause you to feel tense and agitated?

- Which sensory experiences seem to be calming to your child?

- Which sensory experiences seem to be overwhelming for them?

## CREATING A HELPFUL NARRATIVE

Becoming aware of your parenting story is the first step. Rewriting the narrative comes next. You do not have to stay in your current way of thinking. You have the opportunity to break generational molds and parent in a way that fits with your personality, priorities, and values. You can parent free from shame, embracing what makes you unique, believing you are worthy.

Take an answer from the questions above, or identify a belief that impacts your parenting in an unhelpful way. Write it on the left side of a piece of paper. Then revise it on the right side of the page. Write it in a way that is honest, positive, encouraging, and grace-filled. Acknowledge your personality and history. Make note of your challenges in a nonshaming, nonjudgmental way.

It's not easy to rewrite our old narratives. Many are so firmly ingrained in our thoughts, we don't even know they are there. Sometimes they feel so familiar, it's uncomfortable to think about changing them. If you're stuck, think about how you would help a friend rephrase their thoughts or rewrite their story in a positive way.

Here are some examples:

| If your current story sounds like . . . | You can rewrite it . . . |
| --- | --- |
| "Big feelings should be avoided at all cost. Big feelings make me feel anxious." | "Big feelings were minimized in my family growing up. I don't want to do that for my kids. I want to learn how to manage my anxiety and embrace all my kids' big feelings." |
| "Noise really bothers me, but a good mom is attentive to her kids at all times." | "Noise really bothers me. It's hard to listen well when so many people are talking. Pausing the conversation and listening to one person at a time works better for me—and my kids!" |

*(continued)*

| If your current story sounds like . . . | You can rewrite it . . . |
| --- | --- |
| "My daughter's behavior is really challenging. I'm the only one who can help her. I'm exhausted." | "My daughter is struggling right now. I need to find professional support to help us through this difficult stage. I do not need to do this alone." |
| "Parenting is not at all what I expected. I resent the fact that my kids need so much of my time. I'm not cut out for this." | "Parenting is not at all what I expected. I miss my alone time. That is OK. I can find a way to have my own hobbies and be present for my kids." |

If you're feeling overwhelmed, take a deep breath. You don't need to master all this at once. And you don't need to know how to fix it or make it better right away. The rest of the book will focus on giving you skills and strategies to help you blend your story with your parenting in a way that makes you feel calm and confident. For now, give yourself a big hug for doing the difficult work of starting with you.

When we, as parents, take responsibility for our stories, we don't pile unnecessary burdens on our children. We won't do this perfectly all the time. There will be plenty of times when we let our negative thoughts, old beliefs, or impulsive actions get the best of us. Perfection is not the goal. The goal is to move forward in a positive direction, giving ourselves—and our kids—grace upon grace during the process.

Parenting would be much easier if everyone was happy and content all the time, but as we all know, that is not the case. The next chapter will look at ways to embrace emotions—even the big, messy, uncomfortable ones.

## IT STARTS WITH YOU

- What did you learn about yourself through this process?

- What part of your story can you celebrate?

- What support or strategies do you need to help you move forward?

# CHAPTER 4

# No Robot Parents

**"When you feel jealous, talk about** it, and we'll figure something out."[1] The catchy tune makes me smile. Since its debut in 2012, I've been Daniel Tiger's biggest fan. The cartoon created for young children gave parents like me a simple vocabulary to talk (and sing!) about difficult emotions and nuanced social situations with our kids. Whether he was dealing with jealousy over a sibling getting more attention or feeling left out during a playdate, Daniel Tiger's caregivers always have a simple song to help him through.

Unlike Daniel Tiger, most of us had a dramatically different experience with emotions when we were young. Our parents, like the generations before them, had little to no education around emotion identification or emotion management. While most parents (past and present) could name a few basic feelings—sad, mad, angry, happy—the list didn't grow much longer. When a big feeling would show up, we may have been told to "settle down" or "go to your room until you're calm." You may have been told "big boys don't cry" or "you're being too sensitive."

It might not only be negative emotions that were shunned in your history. In some homes, even positive emotions were looked down upon. You may have been told that sharing your achievements was bragging or to stop being so happy because others aren't as fortunate as you.

I don't blame the previous generation for these messages. We are all doing the best we can with the information we have available. Since that time, however, we've come to realize that the best way to help children learn to manage their feelings isn't by bribing them to stop crying or "giving them something to cry about" but by helping them learn to identify and manage their emotions.

## ALL EMOTIONS ARE OK

As an adult, you're carrying around messages about emotions that were formed through your childhood experience. Chances are you have a list of "good" or "acceptable" emotions and a list of "bad" or "negative" ones. You may also have expectations about how these emotions "should" and "should not" be expressed.

I'm going to challenge these long-held beliefs by saying, *All emotions are OK*. As humans, we are created to feel, express, and experience emotions. Even the "bad" or "negative" ones. This means it's OK if your son is angry about his math homework. It's OK if your daughter is anxious about her soccer game. It's OK if your youngest is jealous of her older siblings. It's OK if your son is disappointed that you didn't buy him a candy bar in the checkout line.

And it's OK if you feel these emotions too! You are human, which means you're going to feel a wide range of emotions alongside your children. There's no need to pretend that you don't feel emotions or are somehow immune to feelings.

Though we want to be calm, confident parents, there will be times when our humanity takes over. Even the calmest parent may sense their alarm blaring (see chapter 6) when their kids run through the house with muddy shoes or their child stands in defiance, refusing to comply with a request. It's normal. It doesn't mean anything is wrong with you as a person. It means you're human.

Your kids don't need a robot parent, avoiding all feelings or responding in a neutral tone, even in the most heated moments. They need you to model emotion management, teaching them how to identify their emotions and what to do when these emotions get too big.

But before you can model this, you may need a refresher in emotion identification.

## BUILDING AN EMOTIONAL VOCABULARY

If the thought of teaching your kids about emotions makes you sweat, don't panic. You do not need to be an expert at this overnight. Remember, this is a process of growth and learning. Take it at your own pace.

To begin, start by asking yourself how you feel right now. You don't need to have a word for it yet, simply tune into what's going on in your body and mind. Marc Brackett uses a "Mood Meter" in his work, helping people graph their feelings on a scale of "pleasantness" and "energy."[2]

Let's start with "pleasantness." Some feelings are unpleasant, and we usually want these feelings to go away as soon as possible. This includes emotions like boredom, jealousy, or disappointment. Other feelings are pleasant; we could feel these all day and they would never get old—joy, happiness, love. Take a second to explore how emotionally pleasant you feel right now.

Next, explore your emotional energy level. Some emotions are active and energetic, like when we're excited or angry.

Other emotions don't require as much energy or make us feel slow or sluggish. Low energy feelings may include fatigue or relaxation. How energetic do you feel today?

All feelings can be grouped into categories based on these two descriptors. Some feelings are high pleasantness and low energy, like sitting in front of a warm fire on a cold night. Some feelings are low pleasantness and low energy like trying to get out of bed in the morning after your toddler tossed and turned in your bed all night. Spending the day hiking with friends may leave you feeling high pleasantness and high energy, while running late for your child's school conference may be low pleasantness but high energy.

Again, no right or wrong, good or bad feelings here. Just feelings. Like in the last chapter, the key is noticing—asking yourself questions and being curious about what happened that led to the sensation you experienced. How was your energy level? How pleasant was the emotion? Become more aware of what is going on, rather than being swept away by a wave of emotion or harshly judging yourself for having a normal response to an unpleasant situation.

With time, you can start to put a name to these experiences. It may be helpful to print out a list of emotion words and hang it where you can reference it often. There are many lists of emotions online; some include faces (cartoons and actual images) so you and your children can begin to recognize the nonverbal cues that accompany different emotions. If the feelings are not already separated by pleasantness and energy, you may want to rearrange them in a way that makes sense to you.

Remember, feelings are more than words on a page. They are physical experiences. Your face looks different when you feel worried and when you feel surprised. Your body posture is different when you're tired versus when you're angry. Some feelings are accompanied by physical sensations like dizziness or a stomachache. You may clench your fists, hold your breath, or experience a change in your breathing. Begin to connect the word or image of an emotion to how it feels or looks physically in your body, your child's body, and the bodies of others.

Once you have the basics, you may notice that it's difficult to pick just one emotion at a time. You may be bored waiting in the pickup line after school, anxious about a call from your doctor, pressured by an email from your boss, and delighted by a meme you saw online. We are complex beings living in a complex world. Things are rarely straightforward and simple. As you practice tuning into your own emotions and helping your child identify theirs, give yourself permission to be complex. Like Daniel Tiger says, "Sometimes you feel two feelings at the same time, and that's OK."[3]

Now that the foundation is set, you can build and expand the conversation around emotional identification with your kids as they grow and mature. Your goal is to empower them with information so they can become experts at identifying feelings in themselves and others. The message you want to send is, "As a human, you will feel a wide range of emotions. There is nothing wrong with you; this is normal. Here's the word for what you're feeling. And when you feel a big, overwhelming emotion, I am here to help you learn to manage it in a healthy way."

Here are a few ways to playfully explore emotions with your kids:

- Read books or watch videos of people showing different emotions. Have your child mimic the face they see using a mirror.

- Draw five circles on a piece of paper. Take turns with your child, each drawing a different facial expression inside.

- Pick an emotion from a list and have your child act it out—or better yet, you act it out and have them guess.

- Use TV shows, books, and real-life scenarios as opportunities to practice identifying and naming emotions.

- Draw a simple outline of a person on a piece of paper. Encourage your child to pick a color and show where they feel an emotion in their body. For example, anger may be red, and you may color your arms and chest to signify that you notice anger most in your arm muscles and rapid heartbeat.

- Label the picture with external triggers, conversations, situations, or internal dialogue that correspond with a particular feeling.

## SHINING THE SPOTLIGHT

Of course, we don't want to make excuses for our yelling, blaming, or anxious behavior with our children. As adults, we need to do the work necessary to be the mature ones in the relationship. You've already started this journey in the previous chapters. Congratulations!

Though anger is a human emotional experience, there is often more to the story than just a raised voice and clenched fists. Situations that leave you feeling angry, anxious, controlling, stressed, overwhelmed, frustrated, or panicked are often shining a spotlight on an area of your life—past or present—that needs to be addressed. When we are brave enough to take a step back and examine the situation from a distance, we are often able to see things more clearly.

Here's an example: It's late. Your son had a band concert this evening, so bedtime was delayed. You rushed through baths and teeth brushing. Pajamas were a struggle, but now everyone's ready for bed. Your son, exhausted from the day, is asleep as soon as his head hits the pillow. Your daughter, on the other hand, is having trouble settling down for sleep. She's bouncing on the bed and throwing stuffed animals everywhere.

You do your best to stay calm, encouraging her to settle down for quiet reading time together. You turn off the lights and offer a backrub. Nothing works. She's still as energized as ever. As the minutes tick by, your anger level rises. Without warning, you explode. Setting her on the bed much harder than necessary, you tell her to "go to sleep" and slam the door behind you.

A few minutes later, you hear sniffles and crying behind the closed door. Still a little angry, you go in and demand to know what's wrong now. "You yelled at me!" comes the little voice in the bed. A wave of emotion hits you and guilt floods your senses. This is not the first time you've lost your cool with her—especially at bedtime—and you feel horrible.

Instead of beating yourself up for losing your cool, excusing your anger by blaming your children, or sweeping it under the rug, let's look at a healthy way you can process what just happened.

First, take a few deep breaths. Separate yourself from the situation, giving your brain time to calm down so you can think clearly.

Next, with as much grace as possible, think through the situation without judgment, as if you were an outside observer, rather than someone who lived through it. Make mental notes of the things in the environment, your stress level, thoughts, feelings, past experiences, anything that impacted you and your behavior in the moment. It's OK if you don't have a lot of information here. It's not about having all the answers; it's about being curious.

You may notice yourself thinking, "I was tired, I had a long day at work, and the band concert was loud (and honestly, a little squeaky). I knew I had a sink full of dirty dishes that still needed to be washed, and a few bills to pay. I was really hoping to have some time to relax after the kids were in bed, and this meltdown was really inconvenient. When I was a kid, it wasn't an option to refuse bedtime. If we did, we were spanked without question. At the core of all this, I don't really know how to handle her when she gets like this. I don't trust my parenting, and I feel like a failure." Keep in mind, none of these are excuses; they're all information.

Now you can decide what, if anything, you'd like to explore further. Shining a spotlight on the areas that need work is not a guilt trip or meant to send you into a shame spiral. It's an opportunity. A chance for you to put your energy and resources into an area that may not have been explored previously. Like looking around an old house, some areas may be immaculate, while others may need a good dusting. There's nothing wrong with the house just because a few cobwebs fill the corners.

In the situation above, the parent may realize a few things: busy nights need a condensed bedtime routine. Her daughter may need more help calming down for bed, especially after a fun activity. Which means there may be less time to relax afterward. And as a long-term goal, the parent may need a few new strategies for managing power struggles without yelling.

This is where growth happens.

We have an opportunity to become the calm, confident, mature caregivers our children need when we look at ourselves and our own behavior with curiosity. When we are willing to do what we can to address underlying issues and learn skills that were not taught to us as children.

If emotional identification and management are new to you, welcome! It's never too late to learn something new. Be kind and gracious with yourself as you go forward. Notice times when you hear the whisper of shame messages or when something clashes with your upbringing, culture, or community. Without making a judgment, give yourself time to think it through, talk about it, and explore—accepting all emotions as OK—and then decide how to move forward.

Sometimes, we will parent with grace, ease, and a strong connection with our kids. And sometimes, we will slip back into old habits, overreact, or create a rift in the relationship. The next chapter will give you a plan to move through mistakes without getting stuck in shame.

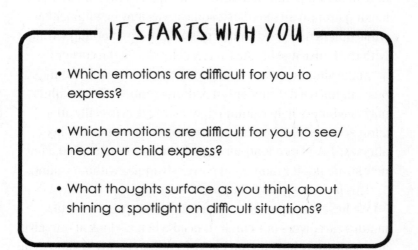

## IT STARTS WITH YOU

- Which emotions are difficult for you to express?

- Which emotions are difficult for you to see/ hear your child express?

- What thoughts surface as you think about shining a spotlight on difficult situations?

# Chapter 5

# When I Make a Mistake

**Let's pause and take a deep** breath. A slow inhale and a longer exhale. Becoming more aware of your present and past story, learning to recognize shame, and naming emotions can be hard work. In time, you may feel more settled into your role as a calm, confident caregiver, but nothing will change the fact that you are human and imperfect. There will be times when you yell, lose your temper, bribe, threaten, give a harsher consequence than necessary, or just close your eyes and wish that the challenges in front of you would all go away.

Both things can be true. You can be an amazing parent and be imperfect. Perfection is impossible and not even worth striving for, so let's give that up right now.

I realize you may be carrying a huge burden into each day of parenting. You may feel an overwhelming amount of guilt about your past behaviors. You may be overcome by shame, believing you are flawed beyond redemption. You may look at your children—age eight months, eight years, or eighteen years—and regret the time that has passed. You may look at your past and feel like breaking free of generational patterns is an impossible task that you will never accomplish. You may look around your home and think, "I can't even get the laundry folded, how will I ever learn to parent my kids any differently?"

To you, I say, you are seen. You are loved. You are welcome here.

It is not too late. Your mistakes and history do not define the path forward. The only thing that matters is your desire to make changes and move forward in a positive direction.

Not perfectly. Not without mistakes, slipups, or regrets.

Just one step at a time. Getting back on track when old habits show up.

## WHAT MATTERS MORE

This book places a lot of emphasis on calm parenting. And for good reason—when we are calm and confident, our kids feel safe and secure. Our actions can encourage positive, healthy brain development, giving them tools to manage difficult situations and big feelings for the long term. Calm parenting allows us to make good decisions and keeps us from getting stuck in situations where we give a random consequence that is impossible to enforce. When calm parenting sets a tone for our homes, it inspires our kids to use strategies they observe from us in their own lives.

We don't need to discuss the negative impact of yelling, angry, passive, disconnected parenting. We are probably all too familiar with those traits in our own parenting. Plus, our brains have what is called a "negativity bias." This means they are hardwired to remember and hold on to negative experiences and situations over positive ones. Many parents spend way too much time beating themselves up for mistakes or analyzing their less-than-stellar parenting moments hours after they've passed. Exploration and curiosity are good. It is healthy to have an idea of why certain situations are challenging for you. It's helpful to know your triggers, but being obsessed with your failures and mistakes can quickly become a self-hatred session.

Just in case you missed it last time, let me remind you: your child does not need perfect parents. They don't need perfectly calm parents, and they definitely don't need robotic, unfeeling parents.

What your children need is a parent who is willing to focus on reconnection and repair.

Disagreements, arguments, and misunderstandings are part of every relationship. In fact, they're unavoidable. How we handle conflict is important. Your go-to response may be to sweep it under the rug, ignore it completely, blame someone else, or hope it somehow resolves on its own. Parenting from a grace-based perspective means learning how to lovingly repair a rift in a relationship. Authors Dan Siegel and Tina Payne Bryson explain the importance of our response after a conflict: "Ruptures without repair leave both parent and child feeling disconnected. And if that disconnection is prolonged—and especially if it's associated with your anger, hostility or rage—then toxic shame and humiliation can grow in the child damaging her emerging sense of self and her state of mind about how relationships work."[1]

Repairing the connection with your child soon after a conflict keeps the relationship strong, models healthy communication skills, and strengthens your child's brain development. What could be seen as a colossal parenting mistake is now an opportunity for learning, growth, and connection with your kids. Amazing!

## HOW TO REPAIR THE RELATIONSHIP

Like everything we've talked about so far, this part of parenting is about you first. We need to be the mature person in the relationship instead of expecting our kids to fill this role. Yes, you'd love to have your daughter recognize her part in the argument. You really want your son to apologize for the things he said. We will get to that. There will be time for teaching and working on new skills, but first we need to rebuild the connection.

When kids feel safe, secure, and connected to their caregivers, they are more open to feedback. They are more willing to apologize and take responsibility. Their brains are calm and ready to learn—this means they'll be more willing to listen to the lessons you're trying to teach! Repair is an essential first step to getting back on track.

It's tempting to rush into forcing apologies, demanding confessions, or creating solutions, but doing so will keep you stuck in old patterns. Instead, keep the relationship front and center. Repairing the relationship with your child is more important than being right, having the last word, or ignoring conflict.

### Apologize

As an adult, it's your job to make the first step and own your part in the disconnection. Keep your apology simple and heartfelt: "I'm sorry I lost my temper earlier. My brain was overwhelmed, and I didn't take time to calm down before I responded." Stay focused on yourself and your behaviors. Resist the urge to add "but you . . ." to the end of your apology. Adding a "but" negates the first part of the sentence and usually makes it about the child's behavior rather than your response. Don't make excuses for your behavior or place the blame on anything or anyone else. It doesn't have to be long, flowery, or even super serious. It can be as simple as, "There I go again, crying over spilled milk! Literally." Then giving your child a hug before grabbing a towel to clean up the mess.

Apologizing profusely, using guilt-filled language, or crying uncontrollably during a conversation with your child can send a confusing message. Your child may feel compelled to take care of you rather than the other way around. They may internalize the conversation, leading to feelings of shame about their role in the conflict. The goal of this step is to model taking responsibility for your actions rather than placing blame on others. It's meant to acknowledge a child's experience and remind them that, even though you make mistakes, you are still confident and able to care for and love them, just the way they are.

Shame can keep you stuck. It can whisper your flaws over and over, making it seem like your apology didn't "count" or convincing you that you need to do more to earn back your child's love. Catch yourself if you tend to apologize over and over for the same infraction. One heartfelt apology is enough. If you find yourself ruminating on the situation for hours or days, it's time to process it with another adult. You may need to talk it through with a friend, a therapist, or your coparent.

Some parents find it helpful to journal about parenting challenges. If you choose to journal, I'd encourage you to share your mistake, and then write a response to yourself in a kind, heartfelt manner. Think about how you would respond to a friend who is in the same situation. Remember, we are often harder on ourselves than we are on others!

A side note about apologizing: you do not deserve to be yelled at, hit, treated badly, or abused. There's a difference between acknowledging your part in a conflict and allowing unhealthy behavior to continue. Taking care of yourself, your safety, and your needs may be an important part of the repair process in the relationship with your child. If you're struggling to know if a situation is unhealthy or if you need support to set healthy boundaries around safety, please seek support from a mental health professional.

## Listen Well

We'll talk about listening in more detail later, but for now, listening well means being willing to set your own agenda aside so you can hear what your child is trying to say. You do not have to agree with your child to offer empathy, to put yourself in their shoes, or to see things from their perspective.

This might mean sitting through some strong language of hurt or pain. Listening well might mean staying calm enough to recognize that your child is struggling to find the emotion that best expresses their experience. Instead of saying, "I felt disappointed when you didn't buy me that video game," they may lash out saying, "You're the worst mom ever!" Rather than taking this to heart or demanding they take it back, you can read between the lines, recognizing that they are feeling big, complex feelings that are difficult to put into words. Author Harriet Lerner says, "Only after we can hear our children's criticism and anger, and are open to apologizing for the inevitable hurts and mistakes that every parent makes, can we expect to be truly heard by them."[2]

*Rebuild Connection*

Repair is more than just offering an apology and moving on. It is about rebuilding a rift in the relationship. We want our kids to know that they are worthy of our time, affection, and attention even when there is conflict. And that their behavior—even behavior that causes conflict—does not make them unlovable.

Reconnecting may look different for each child in your family because each child has their own unique way of feeling seen, known, and loved. Reconnection may mean pulling your child in for a hug, giving them a do-over, offering forgiveness, or sharing a snack. One child may feel reconnected after throwing a softball together in the yard. Another child may feel reconnected after snuggling quietly on the couch, while another may want to hash it out verbally, needing to make sure you hear their side of the story, their hurts, or their experience before being willing to see it from another person's perspective.

You'll have an opportunity to dig deeper into connection in a later chapter, but for now, know that there is no right or wrong way to repair the connection as long as you are focused on keeping the relationship strong.

*Don't Force It*

Just because you attempt to repair the relationship doesn't mean your child is going to joyfully run into your arms accepting your apology and offering their own. We cannot force a child to reconnect with us before they are ready. Rather than apologizing again or forcing an apology from them, just be present. Say something like "I'm sorry I lost my cool. I can see you're not ready to talk yet. That's OK. I'll be here when you're ready." Depending on the child, they may be ready in a few minutes, a few hours, or a few days. In some especially challenging situations, it may take longer. Don't give up! Continue to treat them with respect and kindness, never withholding connection as a punishment. Your presence and willingness to wait until they're ready can speak volumes to your child.

It may be tempting to rush the reconnection process, especially if you've tried to listen and offered an apology. This discomfort can lead us to minimize the child's experience by saying things like "Just get over it!" or "It wasn't a big deal." You may find yourself demanding an apology—only to get a halfhearted one in return. If repair is a new concept in your home, your child may be skeptical that your apology won't turn into a lecture. Or their own shame spiral may make it difficult to talk about their own feelings or admit they made a mistake. The more consistent you are at repairing rifts, the easier it will be for your child to apologize, join in a problem-solving conversation with you, or accept your bids for reconnection.

As reconnection and repair become more of a habit, you can introduce the concept to your children, helping them reflect on the situation, owning their part in the conflict, learning to listen empathetically, and exploring ways to make amends.

But don't get ahead of yourself.

The goal right now is to set the tone for positive repair. To show your children that it's OK to be imperfect, that it's OK to make mistakes, and that rifts can be mended. Before you can teach this to your kids, you may need to practice on yourself, showing yourself grace as you move past your parenting "failures" to repair and reconnection.

I remember a rough morning with my eleven-year-old. I don't know why that morning was more challenging than others, but it seemed like we were battling over the smallest details. We were both upset by the time the bus rolled up to the stop. She got on the bus without looking back or saying goodbye. Normally, this would have hurt, but today, I was still harboring frustration about our morning. Honestly, I didn't feel like saying goodbye either.

I was not focused on repair. I wanted her to admit her part and apologize for the things she'd done to upset me. I wanted her to make the first move.

But as the dust settled and I was able to calm my body and brain, I acknowledged what I already knew: it was my job to repair this disconnection. So I opened my computer and composed an email to her. It took a few drafts, as I had to go back and delete every "but you" reference:

> Just wanted to say sorry about how our morning went. I know you need love and compassion and empathy on busy mornings—not criticism from me. You have a lot going on at school and it's a lot to deal with. I hope today surprises you in a good way! Love, Mom.

I hit send and waited.

Hours later, she replied, "I'm sorry too. Love you, Mom." My heart melted. It wasn't a gushing apology, but it was a step toward reconnection. Our conflict seemed so big at the time. So important. By sending this email, I was able to show her that the rift between us wasn't the chasm it felt like in the moment. I was able to model that, though disagreements are inevitable, they don't have to end negatively. And that no conflict is too big to begin the repair process.

That is my hope for you and your children. Give up on finding parenting perfection and get busy practicing repair.

In the next chapter, we will dig deeper into parenting with a calm confidence, starting by learning about my favorite part of the body: the brain.

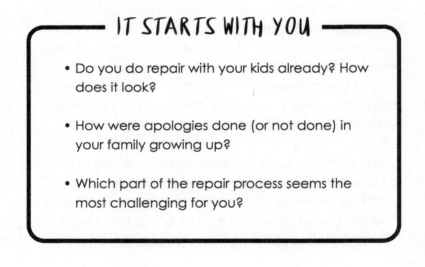

## IT STARTS WITH YOU

- Do you do repair with your kids already? How does it look?

- How were apologies done (or not done) in your family growing up?

- Which part of the repair process seems the most challenging for you?

# CHAPTER 6

# An Introduction to the Brain

**When I began working with children** and families in the early 2000s, brain research wasn't even on my radar. Instead, I sat with concerned parents, huddled around tables making lists of undesirable behaviors and their corresponding rewards and consequences. "If you take out the trash, you'll get a sticker." Or, "If you speak disrespectfully, you'll lose TV time." We created complex token systems, believing that if we just found the right combination of trinkets or just the right consequence, kids would be motivated to follow the rules, manage their big feelings, and make good decisions.

Even then, I knew something was missing. Two weeks into a sticker chart, a child would find a loophole, refuse to do a task unless they were given a sticker, or worse, refuse to do the task at all. I never took into consideration how a child's brain development impacts their behavior, how they are influenced by the environment around them, or how brains change over a lifetime. Little did I know, neuroscientists and neurobiologists were busy working and publishing some amazing research that would forever change the way I thought about behavior and parenting strategies.

Within a few years, I completely abandoned reward charts and parent-created consequences. I now believe that the key to understanding a child's behavior—and our own responses as parents—starts with the brain.

## THE "ALARM SYSTEM"

You don't need to be a scientist to understand the brain. Even a little information can go a long way toward calm, confident parenting. My goal here is to present simple and easy-to-understand information about how the brain functions. This information underlies everything else discussed in this book. We'll come back to it time and again.

We'll start with the amygdala. This is the most primitive part of your brain. It's the first to develop because it plays a crucial role in keeping you safe and alive. I call it the "alarm system." This is the part of your brain that scans the environment for threats and sounds the alarm if it senses danger.

When the alarm sounds, your body prepares for action. Your breathing shallows, your heart beats faster, your pupils dilate, the blood leaves your fingers, toes, and stomach and heads to your bigger muscles, and your body fills with adrenaline. Your brain gets you prepared, in an instant, to fight the threat—or run away, if necessary.

All these preparations are super helpful when you're being chased by a bear or when your child is wandering into a busy intersection. Unfortunately, these are the same biological responses that occur when you feel threatened in mundane situations—like when your children won't brush their teeth or when they refuse to put on their shoes.

That's way too much preparation and adrenaline to handle the more ordinary situations well, bringing us to the first problem with the amygdala: when the alarm is blaring, the thinking, logical part of your brain shuts down. From your brain's perspective, you do not need to be logical when you're facing an immediate threat; you just need to stay alive.

This leads us to the second problem with the amygdala: it's bad at detecting true threats. The brain is going to go through all this prep whether it sees a real threat (like a rattlesnake in your path) or interprets a presumed threat (like assuming that the stick in your path is a rattlesnake). When your child talks back to you, the amygdala may be triggered, turning on the alarm system. The message may be something like "Threat detected: child talking back. React! Respond! Do something!" With the alarm sounding, we're going to parent from panic mode. We're more likely to threaten, spank, and give harsh consequences. We might give in or hide in our bedrooms. We may yell and say things we don't mean.

Over time, using the information in this book, your brain can become more skilled at differentiating between *true* threats and *assumed* threats. You can learn to calm your own alarm before responding to your child, which creates an environment for your child's brain to learn how to calm itself as well. Let's look at a part of the brain that can help us regulate this alarm.

## THE "THINKING PART"

The brain is a hardworking organ with many parts working together to help us stay alive, create memories, store information, and function on a day-to-day basis. Thankfully, we don't need to be brain scientists to use this information in our parenting, so we'll sidestep the immense complexity of the brain and focus on one other specific part: the prefrontal cortex. I call this the "thinking brain" or "thinking part." This is the part of the brain that helps us make good choices. It helps us think through decisions, weigh consequences, and choose a good choice over a not-so-good choice.

Unfortunately, the prefrontal cortex is the last part of the brain to fully develop. In fact, scientists believe that it is not fully formed until we are twenty-five years old.

When your kids are itty-bitty, the amygdala, the "alarm system," is running the show. They feel emotions and react. Some of these feelings are really big. Expecting young children to manage these emotions is not reasonable. They can't. It's nothing you're doing wrong, and it's not a sign that you need to impose stricter discipline. Biologically, their brains are still in a very early stage of development. What they need from you is calm, confident comfort. They need *you* to be their prefrontal cortex, their "thinking brain." Their brains are going to toss you a problem through their behavior. Let's imagine your baby is hungry, so she begins crying. Her brain may be saying, "Mom! I feel hunger! Threat! Threat! I'm panicking!" When you respond to this assumed threat with confident body language and kind words and warm milk, you are able to turn off her alarm and help her brain return to a calm state.

The brain goes through many rounds of growing, learning, and reorganizing by the time we reach our twenties. It's a mistake to think, "My kid's three, he should be able to . . ." or "She's nine, she can think through the consequences by now." Of course, as a child grows, the brain also matures, but this is a long, slow process. You may get glimpses of progress from time to time (thank goodness), but it will be inconsistent. The ability to make a good decision can be impacted by hunger, thirst, over/understimulation, sleep, previous traumas, and whether or not a child feels connected to their caregivers. If your child was up late and she seems to struggle with her behavior the next day, it's not an *excuse* to say, "She's tired." It's a biological fact.

Research also shows that, while all children develop at their own rate, children who are more intense or sensitive may show a delay in emotional development by almost two years. Just because another four-year-old can sit through story time at the library doesn't mean your child can. Or should. All children need unique support as they grow and mature.

For now, I'd encourage you to settle in and get comfy with that fact. Your children are going to rely on you to be their prefrontal cortex for many years to come.

## CHANGING THE BRAIN

One of the most encouraging pieces of information to emerge from brain research is the idea that you can actually change your brain. And your child's brain. This is an amazing opportunity! Not only can we use this ability to create good, healthy habits, this means we can also unlearn negative or challenging habits.

The first step in changing the brain involves the dance between the amygdala, the "alarm system," and the prefrontal cortex, the "thinking brain." When a threat (or a perceived threat) occurs, your amygdala can run it by the prefrontal cortex: "Hey, what do you think about this? Should we panic?" The prefrontal cortex may respond, "No threat here—I can manage it." At first, the amygdala may respond, "Nah, this seems pretty big to me. I think panic is the right response." And alarm bells sound. But with safety, maturity, time, and practice, your amygdala can learn to trust your prefrontal cortex. It can stop its hypervigilant search for possible dangers and threats and let logical thinking take the lead.

Until that time, we'll need to step in and be the "thinking brain" for our kids. Since your child's amygdala is still running the show most of the time, you will have numerous opportunities daily. Here's an example: First thing in the morning, your daughter demands cereal. Unfortunately, she finished her favorite brand yesterday and she's not happy with the choices that remain. Her frustration boils over and she falls to the floor screaming. Her amygdala alarm is sounding: "Threat! Threat! Our favorite cereal is *gone!*" You know that her breakfast choices, while not ideal, are not the threats her brain thinks they are. Taking a big deep breath, you crouch down next to her. "We don't have the cereal you like, huh? It's disappointing when that happens." You're not panicking; you'll find her something to eat eventually. For now, she needs to cry about cereal and cuddle with you.

A few hours later, your son comes home from school tense and angry. He has to redo an assignment for math and he's not happy about it. Instead of completing the assignment, he heads to his video game console and becomes immersed in a game. You cautiously approach him: "Hey, let's take a look at that assignment together." He ignores you. Internally, his brain alarm sounds: "Threat! Threat! Don't let Mom see your grade. Don't let her know that you made so many mistakes. She'll be mad. Avoid! Hide!" Stepping in as the thinking brain, you say, "I know avoiding this math assignment seems easier than facing it. Sometimes we don't get it the first time and that's OK." He is still resistant, but you are calm and confident. Remembering that humor works well in these situations, you make a joke and get him laughing. This lightens the mood as you head to the table to tackle the homework together.

When our kids are melting down ("alarm system" blaring) and we meet them with a calm, confident response (being the "thinking brain" for them), their brains receive this message: "Big feelings mean someone will be there to comfort me. Big feelings come and go. I will get through this." Each time this happens, a new neural pathway is created in your child's brain. The more often we respond in this way, the stronger these pathways become, making it easier for him to manage big feelings in the future.

Changing the brain takes time and practice. As adults, we come into this parenting gig with a number of very strong pathways of our own. Some are not so helpful: "When my child cries, I remember how I was criticized for crying as a child, so I will do whatever I can to get them to settle down. Immediately." Some are helpful: "When I listen to music from my teenage years, my mood dramatically improves. And there's a good chance I'll start an impromptu dance party with my kids."

As a parent focused on grace-based parenting, this is very good news. It means we were created with flexible brains! It means we are not stuck in unhealthy patterns forever, and there is hope for change in the future. Knowing about the brain can also help us respond with empathy when our children struggle. While we could wish their bad behavior away or try to create a reward system to motivate change, the reality is that the brain is a complex organ. It takes time to grow and mature. We can't expect our kids to have fully formed brains. But we are in a unique position as their caregivers to come alongside them, to be their prefrontal cortex as they grow up, and to tell their amygdala, "It's safe. I am here. There's no need to panic."

If our kids are going to rely on us to help them create strong, healthy neuropathways, they need parents with strong, healthy neuropathways. In the next chapter, we learn more about what happens when the brain is in this alarm state.

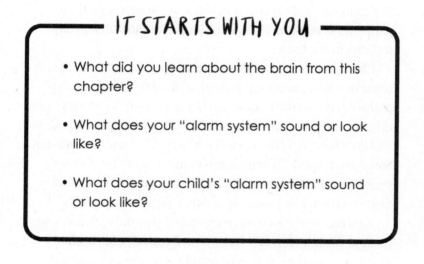

## IT STARTS WITH YOU

- What did you learn about the brain from this chapter?

- What does your "alarm system" sound or look like?

- What does your child's "alarm system" sound or look like?

CHAPTER 7

# When the Brain Feels Threatened

**Family movie nights in our home** aren't always the picturesque bonding times I hear about in other families. Instead of snuggling up under a blanket sharing a bowl of popcorn, we begin our night scrolling through seemingly endless lists of movie options.

Inevitably, one child wants a certain movie. Another disagrees. Two children pick another option only to be vetoed by the third. On our good nights, we can usually agree (or settle) on a movie that most people enjoy.

But then there are the nights when things escalate quickly.

One child accuses another of "always choosing the movie." Someone throws a remote in frustration. Another child responds by hitting back. Someone tries to block, accidentally pushing their sister to the ground.

To say that everyone's "alarms" are sounding would be an understatement.

What do my girls need at this moment? A consequence? A punishment? A lecture?

No.

What they need is a break. Time to let their brains return to calm.

63

I realize this seems passive. Some may say I'm "letting them get away" with this bad behavior. Others may say that what my kids need is a "firm spanking" to "teach them a lesson."

I disagree.

Let's look at this situation from a brain-first perspective.

## FIGHT, FLIGHT, FREEZE, AND FAUN

On the surface, my kids looked like out of control, aggressive attackers. It seemed that they had only one motive—to inflict pain on another person. You may even say that they intentionally hurt others, or that they were trying to "make trouble." And unfortunately, many parenting strategies make these assumptions. But I would like to challenge you to look deeper. To look beyond the observable behaviors and explore what was happening internally.

We already know that the amygdala is the body's alarm system, interpreting the environment and sounding the alarm when a threat is detected. Of course, we also know that the amygdala isn't always great at detecting threats; sometimes it gets it wrong, and very often it overreacts.

Biologically, a brain in threat mode can respond in one of four ways: fight, flight, freeze, or faun. Each of these affects the body's nervous system, creating changes in heart rate, muscle tension, focus, digestion, and more.

For example, in fight, your fists may clench, your arm muscles may get tense, your digestion may slow or stop, your breathing may get shallow, you may have tunnel vision— ignoring everything around you, only focusing on the threat.

In flight, you may feel an intense need to leave the situation at any cost, your lungs may prepare for a sprint, your arms may tremble, and you may be acutely aware of your surroundings.

In freeze, however, your body may feel unable to move. Your muscles may feel heavy, your breathing may change, you may feel sick to your stomach as digestion slows. You may feel lightheaded as oxygen is diverted from your brain to other areas of your body.

A faun response is an immediate desire to please the other person or avoid any conflict. You may struggle to say "no" or set boundaries, and you may feel responsible for the actions and feelings of others.

While the basic biology of fight, flight, freeze, or faun is the same for most humans, how it looks or feels to you will be unique. You may have a go-to response in threatening situations, and sometimes your response will vary. You may find yourself ready to fight when a stranger criticizes your parenting publicly but ready to run away when your own parent criticizes your parenting. Whatever your experience, it's not "bad" or "good" or "right" or "wrong"; it is true for you at that time and place, and that's OK.

Noticing our biological responses from a nonjudgmental perspective is a good place to start. Being able to name when we are in fight, flight, freeze, or faun gives us an opportunity to assess the true threat of the situation and make a calmer decision. The more often we can say, "I'm holding my breath; that's a sign I'm looking for a fight," the better we will be at avoiding the fight altogether. Unfortunately, as adults, we may have years and years of unlearning to do. The biological responses we experience may have been ingrained in us since we were young. Thinking about our bodily sensations may lead us to feel more anxious, depressed, stressed, or panicked. If this is true for you, you may need to seek help from a mental health professional. Again, this is not a sign of weakness, a flaw, or an imperfection. It's a sign that you're willing to do what you need to do to become the healthiest version of yourself.

## BEHAVIORAL RESPONSES

Fortunately, we're no longer battling saber-toothed tigers. The parenting "threats" you encounter on a day-to-day basis may look like your daughter refusing to eat her vegetables, the kids fighting over video games, or your son forgetting his homework assignment. Unfortunately, the brain responds in the same manner whether it's a wild animal or a dropped juice cup.

The brain is programmed to keep us alive. It will do what needs to be done in order for that to happen. The changes that occur in fight, flight, freeze, or faun are biological responses to an assumed threat. At first, these behaviors may feel out of our control and automatic. With time and practice, we can become aware of our body's response to threats, and we can adjust how we respond in these moments.

It's the same for your child.

As you learn to identify your own threat response, be curious about how your child responds when their brain senses a threat. Even if that threat is something you would consider "minor" or insignificant—like being served a sandwich cut in squares instead of triangles.

When your child is in fight mode, their behaviors may include hitting, kicking, hair pulling, spitting, yelling, throwing things, or punching walls.

When they are experiencing a flight response, your child may run away, hide, cover their ears, resist affection, or pull away.

If your child freezes when they sense a threat, they may stay silent, appear unable to respond, become immovable or avoidant, or vomit.

A faun response may lead them to say "yes" and be overly compliant. They may go overboard, being especially cautious not to do or say anything to upset others.

Yes, many of these behaviors are undesirable. Yes, eventually you will want to teach your child different ways to manage their anger and help their brain be a better threat detective. But in this moment, their nervous system is simply responding. Reacting to the alarm.

If we want to parent with grace, we need to start by looking past the observable behaviors. We need to resist the urge to punish or give a consequence for the behavioral responses in times of threat and start to see our kids as needing our help and support to turn off the alarm and get back to calm.

## BIOLOGY NOT DISOBEDIENCE

It is not easy to make the shift from seeing your child's behavior as disobedience to seeing it as a biological response. It's OK if you struggle to comprehend it at first. There is more to the story of a child's behavior, but we need to land here for a while.

The cultural response to behaviors like hitting, kicking, and running away is to search for a consequence. Long-held beliefs tell us that strict and harsh responses are necessary to teach a child not to behave in such a manner. And it's easy to see how we've gotten here. Many children appear to be "obeying" their parents when given a firm warning. If we could see their neurological response, we may notice their brain going into freeze or faun mode, shutting down the observable signs of panic as a way of protecting themselves. They're overly compliant because it seems to be the safer response. Their behavior matches the parent's expectations—they see the child as compliant and obedient—but it doesn't necessarily mean that the child is learning from the punishment.

We want better for our children, right? We want them to actually learn how to manage their big feelings. We want them to learn how to calm their alarms and make decisions when their brain is calm. We want to help them become better at recognizing true threats and filtering out situations that don't need such an over-the-top response.

The best way to start is by seeing these undesired threat responses as biology, not disobedience or defiance. When you see your child as being "disobedient," you are more likely to judge or make assumptions about them or their intentions. You may say things like "She's just trying to manipulate me," or "He's just lazy." When you see your child as being held hostage by their biology, you may have more compassion and empathy for their experience. You may be able to say, "Whoa buddy, you are really upset. I'm here, and I'm going to help you get your brain back to calm."

What a powerful message for the child to receive.

You have an incredible opportunity to support your child. Your child's brain can literally "catch" calm from you. Mirror neurons are a special set of neurons in the brain attuned to the behaviors, routines, and emotions of others around us. This means your kids are constantly looking to their caregivers for cues about how to manage the world. When their brain is out of control and their body is responding in ways that are scary and overwhelming, they look to you for help. This might come in the form of crying, aggression, tattling on their sibling, or simply watching your response. When you model confidence, compassion, and calm, their brain internalizes the message: "My caregiver is there to support me. Big feelings are OK, and I will get through this."

Imagine your child is putting together a LEGO set. The pieces aren't fitting well and his frustration builds. With one angry swipe, the creation is sent crashing to the floor, sending hundreds of tiny LEGOs flying everywhere. If you see his behavior as defiance, your initial reaction may be to say something like "Alex! We do not throw toys. Clean up those LEGOs right now." When he refuses, you may be tempted to send him to his room as a punishment. But if you see his reaction as biology, your response may be different. You recognize his brain was overwhelmed in that moment. He didn't throw the LEGOs to be difficult but as a threat response. Overlooking the explosion of LEGOs on the floor, you focus on modeling calm, confident compassion, "This set is challenging, huh? It's hard when things don't work out the first time." As his brain begins to settle, you gather the LEGOs together, encouraging him to try building the creation again.

He learns that big emotions are a normal part of life and that expressing an emotion, even anger, is OK. You help his brain "catch" calm by keeping your body language, tone of voice, and conversation calm and empathetic. Rather than feeling ashamed, he's more likely to listen to suggestions for managing his LEGO building frustration differently next time.

What an unbelievable gift we can give our children—the willingness to see them as more than their behavior. To see them as children who are struggling and need the support of a compassionate caregiver.

Unfortunately, this may have not been the case when you were a child. You may have been shamed for expressing certain emotions. You may have been punished for reacting to threats by hitting, yelling, or hiding. Your parents may have been focused on creating consequences rather than helping you manage big feelings differently. These experiences may impact how you view your child's behavior and how your brain responds to threats.

As you read about being a calm, compassionate caregiver, you may regret the model you've been up to this point. Instead of providing a confident, "I've got you" message to your kids, your message might be more like "You're panicking! I'm panicking! We're all panicking!"

Those feelings are valid. You can accept these things as pieces of your past without having them define your future.

Remember, we're all imperfect parents. The grace you show your children in the middle of a meltdown is the same grace you can offer yourself. You are unlearning old habits and introducing new ones. You're challenging long-held beliefs and replacing them with new ways of thinking and acting. Of course, it's going to take time, and probably many mistakes, before they become familiar and comfortable.

Take a deep breath.

This is a process, a journey. Start by becoming aware of your own alarm. Notice your go-to response in a threatening situation, even if that situation isn't necessarily a "true" threat. Then notice your child's threat response. Rather than matching it, see if you can offer them calm, confident support. The more often you meet them with this calm confidence, the easier it will be for them to "catch" that calm from you. Slowly, with patience and time, your child will recognize that their brain alarm isn't necessarily a concern but a reminder to turn to you for support.

It's not always easy to know how to respond when our children are upset. The next chapter will walk you through a scenario using calm as our guide.

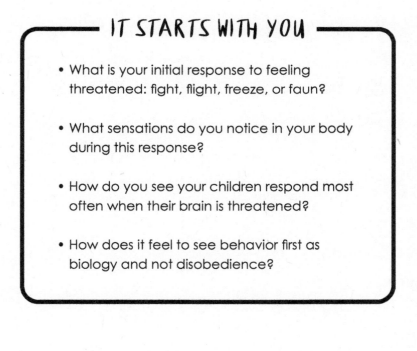

## IT STARTS WITH YOU

- What is your initial response to feeling threatened: fight, flight, freeze, or faun?

- What sensations do you notice in your body during this response?

- How do you see your children respond most often when their brain is threatened?

- How does it feel to see behavior first as biology and not disobedience?

# CHAPTER 8

# The Importance of Calm

**Learning to parent with calm confidence** is the ultimate goal, but the journey to this place may look like a "choose your own adventure" book. I remember reading these books when I was growing up. You begin on page one of the book and read the beginning of the story. Then on page three, you're given two options. If you choose option A, you flip to page ten. If you choose option B, you flip to page twenty-five. Making that one decision, A or B, changes how the story unfolds.

The same can often be true of our parenting. When your child starts to cry, you're given two options: (A) sit down next to them and pull them in for a cuddle, or (B) yell "Settle down!" at the top of your lungs. Both responses will lead to different endings. But unlike a "choose your own adventure" book, where the characters are fictional and there aren't real-life consequences, parenting is always more nuanced than choosing A or B.

As we've already explored, there are hundreds of factors that impact your responses and interactions with your kids: things from your past, sensory overwhelm, your mental health, whether or not you had your morning coffee. And there are hundreds of things that impact your child's reaction to you:

their age, developmental stage, sensory input, ability to self-regulate, and if they slept well the night before.

In any given situation, we have a number of choices as parents: A, B, C, D, all the above, none of the above. The point is not about choosing the "right response"; it's about parenting from a place of calm—or getting back to calm when things get off track—so you can explore all the options available to you.

In chapter 6, we talked about the "alarm" and the "thinking" brain. When our alarms are blaring, the thinking part of the brain goes offline. We're reacting, not responding. We're coming from a place of threat rather than thinking through the situation clearly. In this state, our options seem limited, and we feel trapped, confused, overwhelmed, stressed, and reactive. We're more apt to give a consequence, punishment, or do something we regret. Thankfully, when we turn off the alarm, the thinking brain comes back online. We're able to explore all our options. We can think about our next move, what our children need from us, and creative ways to respond.

This is exactly what our kids need. This is how parenting works best. Being calm and flexible; patient and responsive. Being willing to meet our kids where they are and also managing our own internal frustrations and sensations.

If this sounds like an overwhelming task, that's OK. Take a deep breath. No one is requiring you to master this immediately. Or ever. It's not about perfection; it's about learning and growing over time.

So rather than focusing on discipline, punishment, or finding exactly the "right" words to say, focus on staying calm or getting back to calm. The only person you can control is yourself. That's it! It would be amazing to control your children, but you can't (none of us can). Stay focused on the one thing you can control: you. Yes, that means you need to take your own deep breaths, even when your child does not. You need to take a break before you blow up, even if your kids are still enraged. And you may have to do it over and over and over until it becomes a habit and your child's mirror neurons start to recognize that you are not a threat but a support system.

## PARENTING FROM AN "ALARM" STATE

Here's an example of parenting without taking time to calm the brain.

Within seconds of my daughter's arrival, I can tell something's not right. She said her day was "fine" but threw her backpack on the table with a bit too much force, then slammed the fridge closed when she couldn't find an acceptable snack.

I'm immediately on edge. We've been here before. She gets in these "moods" and sometimes it takes hours before things calm down again. I'm tired, I've had a long day already, and honestly, I don't really have the energy to deal with her negative attitude.

"You don't have to slam the fridge. And pick up your backpack."

"I don't want to," she snaps back. I'm caught off guard by her response. My heart rate picks up, and I can feel a little tension rising in my shoulders. But I know she's had a hard day at school. I take a deep breath.

"OK. So rough day, huh?" I sit in a nearby chair, hoping my change of posture will rub off on her.

"Yeah, it was stupid. Every subject was stupid. I hate school."

"Well, probably not every subject. You love math, right?"

"You never listen! No. I hate every subject. Like I said." She slams her computer on the table. I'm triggered again. I don't like the word "hate" or "stupid," and I think she actually likes school. I don't know why she's giving me so much attitude today. I'm matching her intensity now.

"That's enough. That computer is expensive! You need to take better care of your stuff!"

"What?" She's standing tall now as if challenging me. "I don't take care of my stuff? Have you seen my sister's room? You should be talking to her about taking care of her stuff!"

Apparently, my body is preparing for a fight. I stand up tall too. "We're not talking about your sister. She's not the one slamming things around this kitchen."

From here, I could give out consequences for her tone of voice, her behavior, her disrespect. And she would only escalate, potentially damaging property, hurting herself or others in the process. Which would inevitably be another trigger for me, leading to even more conflict. This cycle would keep both of us in fight or flight rather than putting me in the role of calm, confident, supportive caregiver.

Let's look at how it could go if I focused on keeping my own brain calm first.

## PARENTING FROM A CALM BRAIN

Tension fills the house when she returns home from school. The scowl on her face is all the information I need to know. She slams her backpack on the table and closes the fridge with too much force, and I feel my breath quicken. My jaw sets and my muscles tense.

Thankfully, I notice these warning signs. I take a deep breath, literally biting my tongue to keep from saying something snarky or rude.

"There's nothing to eat," she says, glaring at me.

"We have plenty of food," I reply, then stop before I list the available snacks. This is not going to be productive. Shifting gears, I try, "Rough day, huh?"

"Yeah, it was stupid. Every subject was stupid. I hate school."

Triggered by her words, I feel tension rising again. Another deep breath. I repeat the mantra "This is not an emergency" in my head. I remind myself that she needs empathy, not a lecture.

"Yikes. That sounds awful." I have to force it out; I'm not completely calm yet, but it's obvious she had a horrible day.

"It was!" She stands tall, but not in defiance, more in agreement. "I turned in my homework, but the teacher couldn't find it. She called me to the front of the class and made a fool of me. I was so angry. And embarrassed! I hate her!" Her face becomes red as she recalls the situation.

I don't say anything. I am feeling calmer now; I know what it's like to feel humiliated.

She continues, "Then I couldn't get my locker open, so I was late for gym, and I got points off for the day. It wasn't fair! I was just a minute late!"

I could say something, but I choose to stay quiet, just in case there is anything else she wants to share. Bending down to my daughter's level, I pull her in for a big hug. She stiffens but doesn't push back. I take that as a good sign. After a few seconds, I repeat back, "You had a horrible day. It wasn't fair." Finally, she relaxes into the hug.

Calm, peaceful, slow. Repeat.

"Can I find you a snack?"

"There's nothing to eat," she replies. I sigh, a feeling of frustration rushing through me because she is still annoyed about the lack of acceptable snacks.

"I know." Letting go of our hug, I rub my daughter's shoulders and smile. She needs more time to get back to calm. I can't rush her, even though it would make parenting through this conflict easier for me. I slice an apple and set it on a plate, knowing she'll snack on it eventually.

## MAKING ROOM FOR IMPERFECTION

This conversation could have gone hundreds of other directions. One wrong look, one word, one misinterpretation or misunderstanding could have changed the whole outcome.

Life with kids doesn't follow a script.

The goal isn't to have perfect conversations or to say the right things 100 percent of the time.

Sometimes the words you hoped would be encouraging come across as insulting. Sometimes you talk when you should have listened or stay silent when you should have said something.

There will be days when a deep breath just doesn't cut it, and you lose your cool or feel like giving up. There will still be big feelings, arguments, overreactions, and struggles—from you and your children.

This is normal. This doesn't mean there's something wrong with you or your kids.

It means you have opportunities to learn and grow.

Yes, it would be nice to put this responsibility on our kids. But for now, we, as the confident adults in the relationship, set the tone for productive, calm, and respectful conversations.

When the conversation shifts in a negative direction or your child resists your offers for connection, notice how your body reacts. Begin to recognize the signs that you're heading into fight, flight, freeze, or faun.

Parenting from an alarm state often leads us to feel trapped, stuck, or out of options. Our actions often mirror our child's immaturity. We tend to fall back into old habits like yelling, lecturing, hiding, punishing, or bribing. We may truly not know what to say or do to make the situation better.

Rather than panicking because you don't see another way out, focus on getting your brain back to calm.

When your brain is calm, you will be able to see options you couldn't imagine in the heat of the moment. You will be able to find more empathy for your child's perspective. You may even realize that the thing that seemed so important a few minutes ago is really minor and probably doesn't need the scrutiny you're giving it.

Just like the "choose your own adventure" books, the story isn't over because you make a mistake, or when something you tried didn't work as you hoped. It means it's time to turn the page, take a deep breath, and explore your options. (We will talk more about calming your brain, including tips and strategies to use in those difficult parenting moments.)

Taking care of our own triggers, being responsible for our own behaviors, and deciding to be more mature than our kids isn't easy. Especially if you're breaking generational patterns or are at the beginning of this positive parenting journey.

There is nothing perfect about parenting, and you don't need to handle every situation without making a single mistake. In fact, there is a lot of room for error. The goal is not perfection but moving forward in a positive direction. With time and practice, it does get easier, but life will never be completely free of conflict. Big feelings are a natural part of life, especially life with kids.

So let's say you let your "alarm" system dictate your response. No problem. You're human. Let's go back to the drawing board.

Explore your triggers. Your stressors. Think about what you will say when this situation comes up again in the future. Take a deep breath. Give yourself tons of grace. Give your child a hug. Move forward.

Being calm can be a steep learning curve for us as parents. On exhausting days, we may wonder, "Why is it taking so long for my child to learn how to calm down?" or "When are they going to start making better choices, even when they are upset?" Great questions. To figure out the answer, we need to talk about self-regulation.

## IT STARTS WITH YOU

- How does an "alarm" conversation sound in your house?

- How does a calm conversation sound?

- Do you need to forgive yourself for past "alarm" conversations?

# CHAPTER 9
# Waiting for Self-Regulation

**At about 8:30 p.m., my husband and** I lock eyes across the pool. We know, without speaking it out loud, that we need to wrap up for the night and head home. It's been a long, hot day of swimming, playing with friends, and eating too many snacks. We know our kids are exhausted, and even if they beg and plead for "five more minutes" of swimming, we know that the transition to the car is going to be a challenging one.

We wrap our kids in towels and the crying begins. My five-year-old is wailing, saying she doesn't want to leave and that she's not tired. As we drive away, the frustration intensifies. She starts kicking the seat in front of her. The screaming hurts our ears and everyone begins to feel tense. We do our best to calm her, but nothing works. In fact, some of it does more harm than good. At this point, all we can do is pray that we make every green light on the way home so we can escape the noise.

An overtired child is a challenging child. Their behavior seems irrational and over-the-top. There's no reasoning with them, and logic only exasperates their emotional state. Their behavior can trigger even the calmest parent, causing us to resort to giving consequences or punishments with the hopes it will snap them into "better" behavior. (Or at least behavior that isn't so loud and irrational!)

We long for our children to behave well in overstimulating environments. We can't wait until they can manage difficult situations without overreacting. We are eager for children who are self-controlled and obedient.

What we're waiting for is called self-regulation.

And unfortunately, we often put an expectation of self-regulation on them before they are developmentally ready.

## SELF-REGULATION VERSUS SELF-CONTROL

Describing this process as self-regulation rather than self-control may seem insignificant. But the way we label our children's behavior can impact how we respond. The term "self-control" often implies that our children would be able to manage their behavior better if only they would try harder. When kids struggle to control their behavior, we may see it as a character flaw or, worse, as a reflection of our failures as their parent.

Self-regulation is about learning to manage stress well. It requires that we recognize when we are under stress, have the resources and ability to reduce the amount of stress we feel, or have the skills necessary for getting through the stressful event without having a meltdown.

This is a lot to ask of a three-year-old.

Or an overwhelmed ten-year-old.

And if we're honest, sometimes even a parent at the end of an exhausting day.

If your child struggles to manage themselves well in stressful situations, they are completely on track developmentally. Self-regulation takes time, maturity, and practice, but most importantly, it requires the support of a confident, calm caregiver until it becomes second nature. This is called "coregulation." Instead of expecting your child to "control" themselves, let's focus on controlling ourselves so we can offer support. It's in the context of relationships with regulated adults that kids are able to regulate their bodies, brains, and emotions. And when they learn these skills, the ability to self-control will follow.

Self-regulation is not something your child "should" or "could" master by a certain age. Instead, it is a process of ups and downs, of progress and setbacks. There will be times when you pat yourself on the back because your child managed a difficult situation with poise and times when you shake your head wondering if they will ever learn. Sometimes you'll have both responses within the same hour. Self-regulation relies on brain development, and no matter how hard you try to intervene, your child's brain is going to develop at its own pace.

Thankfully, you're not entirely at the mercy of time, waiting until your child is twenty-five and has a fully formed brain. There are plenty of things you can do in the meantime that will encourage your child to strengthen their self-regulation skills.

## BEING CURIOUS ABOUT STRESS

First, we need to set aside any preconceived notions about what "stress" means. We may think of stress as a looming work deadline or having to keep track of our kids at a busy playground. But for a growing child, we need to expand our definition, including things in their environment like noises, smells, and lighting. Wearing uncomfortable fabric, spending the day in a school classroom, or having too many activities or not enough stimulation can be stressful. Lack of sleep, constipation, ear infections, hunger, thirst, or feeling disconnected from a caregiver can all impact a child's ability to self-regulate.

Starting from a place of curiosity, we can step back and wonder why our children are struggling. We can explore the situation and look for potential stressors, even if we don't feel stressed. Other children their age may seem to be managing the situation without a struggle. Stress is a unique experience. Every child will have a different threshold for the amount of sensory input, conversation, recreation, and emotional experience their body can manage well. And—not to stress you out, but—this threshold can change from day to day!

Most of the time, my five-year-old can leave activities without crying and kicking the car seats. And then there are busy pool days or times when we wait too long to eat lunch when she cannot. It's not that she is "bad" or "disobedient" or that I am a failure as a parent. It's that in this moment, on this day, the sensory and environmental stress was more than her brain and body could manage well.

Yes, even at this age.

There's a tendency to expect more than our children are capable of simply because we think they "should be able" to manage it by now, especially if they've done it well in the past. Sometimes your toddler will be able to "use their words" when they are upset, and sometimes they will fall on the floor, crying, because the stress of identifying and formulating coherent words is beyond what their body and brain are capable of in that moment.

Most of the time, your nine-year-old is an easygoing, carefree kid. But the day after a sleepover is a whole different story. She is irritable, argumentative, and grumpy. Staying up late the night before means she feels exhausted, and that added stress makes it difficult to stay regulated.

Your teenager may be able to problem-solve well most of the time, but during finals week, he is snippy and short-tempered. The stress of studying, lack of sleep, and pressure to keep his grades up pushes him beyond his ability to regulate well.

Even as adults, we know that there are days when the expectations, sensory inputs, activity levels, or energy levels make it difficult to be the calm, confident caregivers we strive to be. Self-regulation gets easier as we get older, but it's never something we achieve with 100 percent perfection.

Putting away the "shoulds" will help you keep an open mind about your child's stress level, recognizing that managing stress well is a skill that takes time and maturity to attain. Your role will change as your child grows, but the goal is always to provide a safe place for your child to identify stressors and learn to manage their stress well.

## ZONES OF REGULATION

The concept of "regulation" may be difficult to understand, and even more difficult to explain to your child. Thankfully, Leah Kuypers, an occupational therapist, designed a program called the "Zones of Regulation."[1] Her work helps us visualize stress, tune into our bodies, identify our emotions, and encourage movement toward calm again. Using the "Zones of Regulation" with your kids gives your family a common language to talk about big feelings without shame.

The "zones" are defined by different colors: blue, green, yellow, and red. Each color correlates with bodily sensations and specific emotions.

Red Zone
Yellow Zone
Green Zone
Blue Zone

Blue is a low-energy color. When you are in the "blue zone," you may be tired, sick, bored, or sad. Your body may move slowly, you may feel like sleeping, or you may have difficulty getting motivated.

Green is a calm and engaged color. When you're in the "green zone," you're feeling happy, content, and ready to learn. This is the state you're in when you're feeling regulated. While there is nothing wrong with any of the colors, this is the color you want to return to after feeling dysregulated.

Yellow is more energetic than green. In this zone, your child may be silly, irritated, scared, or excited. This can be an "alarm" state for some children. It can also be a fun, happy experience, say when your child is eagerly waiting to open a birthday gift.

Red is the most intense version of the zones. Your child's body may be in an alarm state—hitting, fighting, yelling, or crying. They may be so wiggly or silly that you're worried someone is going to get hurt. You may label your child's behavior as "out of control" when they are in the red zone.

Everyone experiences these zones. It's a normal part of the human experience. It is not "bad" to be in the red zone or "good" to be in the green zone. This is about learning to notice which zone we are in and adjust if necessary.

Begin by introducing your kids to each color. As you give a quick overview, see if they can remember a time when they were in each zone. Help them tune into how their body felt at that moment. If you're working on emotion identification, see if you can label the feeling. Name sensory experiences, activities, or other stressors that accompany each color. The zones will look and feel different for each child, and that is OK. For one child, sitting quietly on the couch may mean they are in the "blue zone," while it is a "green zone" behavior for another. The more often you refer to the zones, the easier it will be to incorporate them into your conversations: "It looks like you're in the yellow zone" may be more helpful than yelling, "Settle down!" Or, you can ask, "Which zone are you in right now?" which gives the child the opportunity to practice noticing and naming their experience.

Remember, self-regulation is a process that relies on having a strong relationship with a calm, confident caregiver. Sometimes, you may be able to problem-solve together with your child: "It looks like you're in the yellow zone right now. What can we do to get your body back to green?" But often, kids do not have the insight, experience, or calming skill toolbox needed to make this transition without your support. Rather than expecting your child to recognize their zone or know how to get from the "red zone" to the "yellow zone," focus on yourself. What do you need to get back to green? Once you're calm, you can comfort your child: "I know it's scary to feel out of control. I'm here to help. Let's take a big deep breath together." We will talk more about calming strategies in the next chapter.

It Starts with You

For now, keep in mind that it's normal for your kids to still need your help to regulate their big feelings. In fact, coming alongside your kids when they are dysregulated is the best way to encourage them to grow in this area.

The goal isn't to label the zones correctly or to stay in one zone forever, never experiencing another color. The goal is to empower your family, helping everyone—kids and adults— to recognize when they are dysregulated, and giving options for getting back to calm.

If this seems overwhelming, complicated, or if your child's struggles seem to be bigger than this simplified suggestion can address, please seek support from a mental health provider or occupational therapist. You do not need to do this alone. There are caring professionals willing to come alongside you to support your child as they learn skills and grow in self-regulation.

## WHEN YOU STRUGGLE WITH SELF-REGULATION

As you read about self-regulation, you may find yourself wondering how to come alongside your child to help them regulate when you can't even manage your own big emotions.

If you can relate, you're not alone. Most of us were not taught how to identify and manage stress. Many of us grew up in homes where emotions were minimized (or ignored) and we were expected to figure things out on our own. Some people grew up in traumatic situations where it was unsafe to let their guard down at any moment, and many still live in a constant state of vigilance and caution.

Like everything in this book, there is no perfect way to regulate your own emotions or some achievement level you need to master to be a good parent. Learning about your own emotions, your own stress, and what helps you feel calm again will help you support your child. Doing your own work first is an important part of the process, but you may not be able to do it alone. If you find yourself stuck, it may be time to seek support from a mental health professional. Sometimes, it takes an outside perspective to help us recognize old patterns, to help us identify and name emotions, and to learn what is happening in our bodies and brains. With their support, we can begin to see our child's behavior in a developmentally appropriate light.

Reframe your own challenges in a new way. Rather than beating yourself up about not having enough "self-control," remind yourself that you are learning to regulate. Congratulate yourself when you notice your stress level or name your emotion. Each time, you're moving in a positive direction.

Regulating your emotions while your child is dysregulated is not easy. In fact, it may be a completely new concept for you. And that is OK. The next chapter will walk you through how to work through stress and add a little more calm to your life.

## IT STARTS WITH YOU

- What did you learn about self-regulation?

- What situations or sensory inputs make it difficult for your child to self-regulate?

- What situations or sensory inputs make it difficult for you to self-regulate?

# CHAPTER 10

# Completing the Stress Cycle

**A few years ago, my husband** broke his ankle and ended up homebound for two months. Prior to this, we shared many day-to-day tasks like running to the store and school pickups. We also split childcare; I went to work in the afternoon and evenings once he got home. Overnight, our daily routine was shifted. He couldn't drive. He couldn't walk up and down the stairs. He couldn't do much more than sit and watch as we carried on with homework, meals, and bedtime routines. Like any sudden change, this added an enormous amount of stress to our family.

A few weeks in, I had a thought that shocked me: I want to go for a run.

What?!

I am not a runner. I do not run for fun. I do not own clothes to run in or shoes that accommodate a pace faster than walking.

And yet there I was, thinking about running.

Not only thinking about it but feeling as if I *needed* it.

And so, I started running. I downloaded a couch-to-5K app and (loosely) followed it for the next few weeks. I never fell in love with running. And I didn't turn into an ultramarathoner.

But during that time, the stress was more than my body could process. My brain and body knew that I needed a physical outlet. Something more intense than my usual yoga routine or a short meditation.

Authors Emily and Amelia Nagoski call this "completing the stress cycle."[1] Doing something that lets your body know the threat has passed and you are safe enough to relax again. Exercise is their number one suggestion, followed by deep breathing, reaching out to friends, crying, laughing, and being creative. Unfortunately, many of us are stuck in this stress cycle, never giving our bodies the "all clear" signal. Instead, we forge ahead, pushing our emotions, needs, and wants aside, serving our kids, coworkers, and communities with our brains and bodies operating in the alarm state. It's only a matter of time before we burn out.

Maybe you're familiar with that feeling.

## CALMING STRATEGIES FOR YOU

You may have no idea what is calming for your brain and body. You may have never experienced calm in a way that felt safe and healthy. You may have an Instagram-worthy image in your head of what calming is "supposed" to look like but no idea how you'd put that into practice. (A girls' weekend at the spa? I can't even go to the bathroom alone.) You may have tried a few things in the past but didn't feel like they did any good or were very effective. All those reactions are normal.

Before you decide that calming "doesn't work" for you, I'd encourage you to set aside your preconceived notions and experiences, and give yourself a chance to explore calming strategies from a new perspective.

What will help your body move through the stress cycle? How can you give your body the "all clear" signal, allowing you to turn off your alarm and be calm, confident, present, and relaxed? What activities, sensory experiences, environmental cues, and communities do you need to feel like the best and healthiest version of yourself?

The answers may look different depending on the stage of life you're in right now. Finding a way out of the stress cycle may require some creativity and open-mindedness.

Moving your body is an excellent way to decompress, but you can't leave your toddler home alone while you go for a run. Exercise in this stage may mean online videos with kids running around the room with you.

An hour-long conversation with a friend may be a thing of the past, but you can use a voice memo or video app to send quick messages to each other throughout the day.

Maybe you can't sit at the canvas and paint for hours, but you can join your kids while they play with watercolors at the kitchen table.

Instead of having a peaceful quiet time before your kids get up in the morning, you may decide to prioritize a few five-minute meditations throughout the day.

If you're still unclear about what calming looks like, don't panic.

Start by noticing. Pick an activity to try, then give yourself time to tune into your body. Ask yourself questions like "Do I feel more relaxed doing this activity?" or "Where in my body do I still feel tense?" You can also use a rating scale: one to five, one being totally calm and five being extremely tense. Rate yourself before and after using a calming strategy and see if any patterns emerge.

The questions below are meant to get you thinking outside the box about things that may help you stay calm, return to calm, or complete the stress cycle. There are many different ways to calm your brain and body. You are unique. What works for one person may not work for you and vice versa. The goal here is to explore, notice, and be curious about ways you can practice adding calm to your life. The more often you practice calm, the easier it will be for your brain to recall it in times of stress.

- How can I move my body for at least twenty minutes today?

- Do I need to add stillness or activity? What type of activity? How can I create stillness?

- Do I need to be with people or alone? Which people do I need to connect with?

- Are there areas of my health that need attention?

- How do I need to process my thoughts? By talking, journaling, or drawing?

- Do I have time to do this now, or should I schedule a time to do it later? If later, when?

- Do I need support from a mental health professional, friend, or mentor?

- Which of my senses seems most overwhelmed? What can I do to decrease sensation overwhelm?

- Which of my senses seem to respond best to calming stimuli?

- Which activities make me feel most calm? Which make me feel most agitated?

- Which room of the house makes me feel most calm? Which is the most stressful? Why?

- Which piece of clothing makes me feel most calm? Which is most constricting, itchy, or uncomfortable?

- What colors are most soothing? Which are not?

- Which foods bring comfort? Which foods have negative associations?

- Which scents bring positive memories? What scents are more negative?

- What types of touch are most appreciated? From whom? What types of touch make me feel on edge or uneasy? From whom?

- What phrases are most encouraging and uplifting? Which bring me down?

- Is there a helpful mantra or Bible verse I'd like to remember?

- Is there a visual image—real or imagined—that helps me feel calm?

- What type of music is most soothing? Which is most irritating?

- Which apps bring you a sense of calm? Which ones add stress?

- Which TV shows, podcasts, YouTube videos, books, magazines, or other visual media are encouraging, uplifting, or calming? Which increase a sense of comparison, conflict, or stress?

You may find that just clearing the clutter off the coffee table helps lighten your mood. Or stepping outside for ten minutes in the sunshine does the trick. You may find that the elastic band on your pants is annoying, and it's time to put on your comfy clothes. Sometimes, though, you may find that you are so entrenched in the "stress cycle" that you need the support of a mental health provider to move through it. Acknowledging the need for outside support is a positive step in the right direction.

You may be surprised by what works and what doesn't work for you. During some seasons in our lives, we need a certain type of calming activity, while during other seasons, this type of calming is impossible. Remind yourself that there is no one way to calm that is right for everyone and no one way to calm that will be right for you in every situation.

If finding a calming strategy is more difficult than you thought it would be, you're not alone. Give yourself grace during this process of discovery.

## WHAT DOES CALM MEAN TO YOUR CHILD?

Just as each adult is unique, each child has their own way of getting back to calm. What works for one of your children may not work for the other. As you explore what works for you, it will also be important for you to explore what works for each one of your children individually. I know it would be easier to implement one calming strategy for the whole family, but each person's brain is wired differently. And each will need their own unique blend of calming resources.

Most kids have no idea what a calm body feels like. Telling them to "calm down" is meaningless without giving them tools to use. Even asking a child to "take a deep breath" may be a confusing concept.

Start by becoming a calming strategy detective. If your child is old enough, involve them in this process. In the last chapter, we talked about helping our kids tune into their bodies using the Zones of Regulation. Now we'll add specifics about moving from red to yellow, yellow to green, or blue to green. The more you can empower your child to tune into their stress and take ownership of their calming strategies, the better they will be at self-regulating.

Talk about things in their environment that make them feel calm. Explore sensations that are calming—and that are alarming. Practice high-energy activities like jumping on a trampoline or running around the yard and slow activities like blowing bubbles. Use the list above to get you thinking or notice things about your child's personality or temperament.

Go online and search through calming or coping activities; note anything you would like to try with your child. Gather the necessary items and schedule time to practice during the day.

Of course, like everything we've discussed so far, this process takes time. Your kids may not willingly gravitate toward a calming activity. They may still look to you to help their brain return to calm. One day, they may use a calming strategy instead of engaging in an argument with their sibling. The next day, they may rip up their sibling's paper in anger. This is normal. Choosing to use calming skills consistently takes repetition, practice, and maturity. Celebrate when it happens, and see the rest as room to grow.

## WHAT IF CALMING STRATEGIES DON'T WORK?
Sometimes we try everything to help our children calm down, and they are still upset. At this moment, you may feel sad, frustrated, exhausted, or embarrassed. It's normal to want our children to get back to calm as soon as possible. No one wants their child to be upset, and no one likes feeling powerless to help.

Rather than seeing your child's difficulty calming down as defiance, recognize that returning to a calm brain and body takes time. A big feeling, or meltdown, can last an average of twenty minutes. And many children take much longer to completely return to calm. Some situations make it easier for a child to calm their body, while other environments make it more difficult. Some children struggle to manage sensory input and need extra support from professionals to learn how to feel more control in their big feelings.

Imagine emotions as a hill. At the bottom of one side is the calm right before the big feeling. The hill is your child's emotions and behaviors increasing in severity or intensity. The top of the hill is when their emotions reach their peak intensity. And the far side of the hill is your child relaxing and returning to their baseline level of calm.

Many parents do whatever it takes to keep the ground level, avoiding emotional hills at all costs. It may seem easier to bribe or distract their children at the first sign of a big feeling. Unfortunately, this prevents them from learning how to recognize and manage big emotions when they show up in the future. Feelings are part of life. Rather than smoothing the path in front of your child, get ready to support them as they tackle their emotional ups and downs.

The best time to use calming strategies is either before your child gets to the top of the hill or as they begin to come down. But remember, not every calming strategy will work every time. If your child resists taking a deep breath or getting a drink of water, don't force it. Allow your child to feel a range of feelings—even anger and frustration. Offer your support, connection, and comfort as your child allows in the situation. Let them know you're ready to help them calm down when they're ready.

Don't be alarmed if calming interventions don't work at the top of the hill. At this moment, your child's alarm system is blaring, and it sees everything as a threat—even kind gestures. Your job is to manage your own big feelings, staying regulated so you can guide your child back to calm.

This may be one of the most challenging parenting strategies in this book. Supporting your upset child may bring up many emotions, memories, and sensations. That is OK! We're not robots; we're human. Rather than feeling like this should be "easy" or that your child "should" have this mastered by now, just pause. Take a deep breath. Verbalize what's going on. Be kind to yourself. Use your own calming strategy (or more than one). Go for a run. Call a friend. Chances are, supporting a child through big feelings was not modeled to you when you were young (in fact, the opposite may be true). You're entering new territory. You don't need to be an expert now. Or ever.

The next chapter will build on the calm foundation you've set, changing our focus to connecting with your kids. But don't feel rushed to continue reading. Learning how to calm your brain and complete the stress cycle may be the best use of your time and energy right now.

Remember, this is grace-based parenting. Grace for your kids, but maybe—more importantly—grace for yourself, especially in difficult parenting moments.

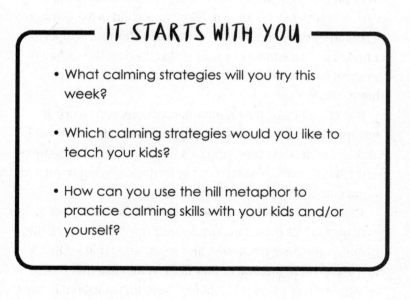

## IT STARTS WITH YOU

- What calming strategies will you try this week?

- Which calming strategies would you like to teach your kids?

- How can you use the hill metaphor to practice calming skills with your kids and/or yourself?

# CHAPTER 11

# An Introduction to Connection

**We found the baggies everywhere.** In drawers, in boxes, in closets. Small baggies filled with nature—sticks, rocks, leaves, pine cones. Sometimes they were labeled in the scratchy, misspelled handwriting of a four-year-old. As she came across nature—a smooth rock—she would exclaim, "I found another rock for my connection!" and joyfully seek out the baggie containing smooth rocks. My daughter called them "connections." It was a mispronunciation of the word "collections," but it seemed fitting (plus, it was cute) so none of us corrected her.

In her little world, everything belonged. And everything was loved.

I can't think of a better way to describe connection.

Researcher Brené Brown describes connection as "the energy that exists between people when they feel seen, heard, and valued; when they give and receive without judgment; and when they derive sustenance and strength from the relationship."[1] This is the message we want to send to our children: you belong, you are valued, and you are loved.

We were designed for connection. As humans, we were not intended to live as individuals without a community of support. We thrive when we have unconditional love, attention, grace, and conversation with others. Unfortunately, our busy society values independence, and we have retreated into our homes and lives, separating ourselves from others, or creating community entirely behind a screen. It's easy to forget—or underestimate—the importance of connection.

But often, we feel it. Without being able to name it specifically, we feel a nagging sense of stress and overwhelm. We worry if we're doing the right thing or wearing the right thing. We compare ourselves to what we can see on the outside of others, usually deciding that we do not measure up. The conversations we have with neighbors, and even friends, are superficial and surface-level. We don't feel safe sharing our worries, fears, and insecurities. And so, we retreat further inside our own lives, often feeling like an outsider, someone who does not belong.

Maybe you never felt a true sense of connection. Maybe your family of origin did not create a safe place for you to grow and flourish. Maybe you were explicitly told you did not belong or did not measure up. Maybe connection is something you tried to create or longed for, only to be hurt or rejected. You may be someone who was valued for never needing anything or for your rigid independence, and the notion of "needing" connection seems foreign to you.

Your experience of connection in your present or past is important. It will impact how you think about, create, and value connection in your family. Like any topic in this book, if connection is a triggering or challenging experience for you, I would encourage you to seek the support of a mental health professional. There is absolutely no shame in seeking help to unravel old beliefs and create a new, healthy outlook and ability to create—and receive—connection.

## HEALTHY BRAINS NEED HEALTHY CONNECTION

From birth, our kids are looking to us to answer the questions, Am I seen? Am I heard? Am I valued?

When the answer to these questions is yes, our kids feel safe and relaxed. They are ready to learn, rest, explore, grow, and play. Connection is the bridge that allows for healthy development and brain growth.

We want our children to learn how to regulate their emotions and manage difficult situations without having a meltdown, talking back, or becoming aggressive. As you know, this is not something that happens overnight. It takes time for a child to gain the ability to regulate their emotions with maturity. In the meantime, you can help your child strengthen their brain (and encourage regulation) by focusing on connection before correction.

Let's imagine your child is learning to ride a bike. He is focused and working hard to figure out how to pedal and keep his balance. Suddenly he tips over, crashes onto the sidewalk, and starts to cry. You rush over to see if he's hurt, but he lashes out at you, blaming you for the fall. He's obviously dysregulated at this moment. His brain is in alarm mode, fight or flight. He's not thinking clearly; he's purely reacting.

Your first response may be to address his angry reaction: "Don't point the finger at me, young man." Or, you may launch into a lecture using logic and reasoning to explain why he fell. At this point, your child may fight back or give up, abandoning the bike altogether.

Instead, let's start with connection.

Getting down to his level, you draw him in for a hug. You inspect his injuries. Then you try to see things from his perspective, being empathetic, letting him know that you understand his frustration: "It's discouraging to fall again. You're working so hard." He nods in agreement. Straightening his helmet and patting him on the back, you help him lift up the bike and encourage him to give it another try.

While we can't rush our kids into maturity, we can encourage less intense reactions, create opportunities to practice regulation, and help build a stronger brain when we make connection our first response. Dan Siegel states, "Neurons that fire together, wire together."[2] A neuron is the part of the brain that transfers information. Within a growing brain, there are numerous connections happening every second. When the brain learns a new and important skill, the necessary neurons in the brain connect or "fire" together. If this skill is repeated often, the neurons "wire together," creating a smooth path to remember this skill faster and more effectively the next time. Every time you use this skill, the pathway becomes more and more ingrained until, eventually, it's automatic. Something you don't even have to think about.

When you respond with connection, you can help your child's neurons "wire together."

Here's how it works. When your child feels a big feeling, the alarm sounds, and they head into fight, flight, or freeze. Their amygdala is in charge, and the message in the brain is *panic*! The body shifts into panic mode, doing what it needs to do to keep your child safe from the threat (real or imagined). These behaviors may be aggressive—hitting, kicking, spitting—or your child may shift the blame, refuse to take responsibility, ignore you, or run away and hide.

If you respond with calm confidence, proving security, love, and acceptance—even in these challenging behaviors—the neurons in your child's brain make a connection. The message your child receives is, "When I feel a big feeling, my caregiver is there to support me. Even though these feelings are big, scary, and overwhelming, I can get through this with their help." Congratulations, the neurons between big feelings and comfort fired together! If this is your go-to response the majority of the time, these neurons will create a strong pathway in your child's brain.

As this pathway becomes stronger, your child may start to recognize that big feelings come and go. They may feel more confident in their ability to get back to calm—even when you are not present. With time, their response may be less intense, their meltdowns may be shorter, and they may return to calm quicker.

Connection before correction may be a new concept to you. Many parenting strategies emphasize the importance of "teaching the child a lesson" immediately. You may be used to creating consequences or doling out threats in response to a child's big feelings. Connecting may feel like "giving in" or "being too soft." You may worry that it's too late to create a healthy pathway because you've never prioritized connection. Or you may just feel tired, wishing that your kids didn't need so much support to make it through their big emotions.

It's OK for this to be a learning process. Like everything in this book, you do not need to master this right away. Or ever. There will be days when your first reaction is frustration, annoyance, or anger. There will be days when you give a lecture when you should listen or threaten when you should have empathized. Be kind to yourself as you figure out how to respond in a way that keeps the relationship strong.

You cannot take away or avoid every situation that may cause sadness, frustration, heartbreak, or irritation, but you can support strong, healthy brain growth by connecting with your child in difficult moments rather than looking to punishment, threats, or consequences.

When your son fell off his bike and pointed the finger at you as the cause, the observable behavior appears to be deliberate belligerence. But underneath these behaviors is often a question: "Am I still loved?" Even though we will never do it perfectly, our goal, as imperfect grace-first parents, is to prioritize the connection over correction. We want our message to be clear: you are loved, valued, and seen in this family. You belong.

## FINDING A PLACE TO BELONG

Thinking about creating strong neural pathways in your child's brain may sound easier than creating community in your own life. It's often difficult to find time to make friends when you're raising children, working, running a home, caring for elderly parents, and volunteering. The thought of reaching out to others may make you cringe. Being vulnerable with a group or individual can be risky, especially if you've been hurt in the past.

Still, if you believe we were created for connection, if you believe that connection—feeling loved, valued, and seen—is important for your children, it is also important for you.

I know that may feel like a leap. It may be easier to brush it aside, focusing only on your kids and ignoring your own need for belonging.

If that's how you feel right now, you're normal.

One of my most precious connections happened after we moved to a new city. My daughters were four and three years old at the time, and knowing no one in the area, we spent our days doing any free activity we could find. One afternoon, during library story time, I spied another mom with children similar to my daughters' ages. I'm an introvert—making small talk does not come easily to me—and I'm certainly not used to approaching random strangers in libraries, but that day, my desire for connection overpowered my loneliness. I approached the mom and asked (in so many words) if she wanted to be my friend. She said yes!

There was a risk involved: What if she judged me for being so forward? What if we had nothing in common? What if our kids didn't get along? What if she lied or talked about me behind my back or rejected my request?

But there was also hope: What if she sensed the desperation I felt? What if our kids also found connection with one another? What if she spoke truth, encouraged, comforted, and supported me?

What if she also needed a friend?

Think about the connections you have in your own life. Where do you feel the most accepted and supported? By whom? Where do you feel judged or disconnected? Who sends these messages? How can you build strong, healthy relationships in your community? Where can you step out of your comfort zone and be vulnerable? What support do you need to build healthy connections or address the disconnections in your community?

The answers to these questions may not come easily. You may need to sit with them for a while before you have clarity. You may need to think creatively about places to make connection. You may need to make difficult changes in your circle of friends. If you feel stuck, unsure, or overwhelmed, talk with a mental health professional. You do not need to process this alone.

Not every random encounter with a stranger will lead to a lifelong friendship, but sometimes it's worth the risk. Parenting can be an exhausting experience. The demands can be more than you can manage on your own. Sharing life with another person or group of people can give you the strength to try something new, stay accountable to a goal, or fill you up so you have more than enough energy and compassion to give your children.

Regardless of your history, your challenges, and your life experiences to this point, you belong.

Maybe you've never heard it before. Maybe you've never believed it. But you are loved, valuable, and seen just because you're you.

Not because you're perfect or doing all this parenting stuff right. Simply because you exist.

The next chapter will help you add moments of connection with your kids, even on your busiest days.

## IT STARTS WITH YOU

- What words or phrases did your child/children say incorrectly but were so cute you didn't correct them?

- What skills has your brain "wired together"?

- How do you feel about your own connection to others right now?

CHAPTER 12

# Connection
# in Real Life

**We are a family of readers.** At any moment, I have four or
five books in progress. My oldest daughter feels anxious if she
doesn't have a handful of books to choose from when she has a
spare moment. My younger daughters dig into one book series
at a time, reading nothing else, until those books are complete.

Reading has always been a big part of my parenting
personality. I'm not a carefree, run-around-the-park kind of
parent. I'm not especially imaginative or creative when it
comes to crafts or make-believe. And I don't always have the
patience to sit on the floor with Barbies or Matchbox cars.

But reading, I can do.

Every night, from the time they were babies, we snuggle
together around a book while I read out loud, sometimes
reading way past bedtime so we can finish the chapter or
not end on a cliffhanger. In these moments, I feel close to my
children. It's quiet and peaceful (most of the time). And no one
needs anything from me, except to hear the words on the page.

But I know my children wouldn't always choose reading
as a way of feeling close to me. One daughter needs snuggles,
hugs, backrubs, physical contact with me. One daughter needs
my full, undivided attention, listening ears, and engaged

conversation. One daughter needs time together, no agenda, just close proximity—not always cuddling, not always talking.

Even though I'd rather just sit down and read a book together, I realize it isn't always going to meet my kids' need for connection. I need to make sure they feel loved, seen, and valued throughout the day in a way that works for them.

## GETTING STARTED WITH CONNECTION

The goal of connection is to consistently remind our kids that they belong. The things we do should help them feel safe to relax, play, rest, and grow. Connecting with your kids doesn't mean an all-day outing to the zoo or buying them the latest and greatest (and most expensive) toy. There is nothing wrong with big adventures or material gifts. These can be fun, memorable, and even bonding experiences. But when we think about prioritizing connection in our home, we want to focus on things we can do on a consistent basis—daily, if possible. Sometimes even multiple times a day. I love the zoo, but I definitely do not want to go there every day.

Creating an atmosphere where our kids feel loved, valued, and seen may seem like an overwhelming task. You may feel stressed, worried that you haven't focused on connection enough, or like you have no idea where to start. Those feelings are valid. Thankfully, it is never too late to focus on connection. Your kids, like all of us, are longing to know that they are accepted and that they belong.

Connection doesn't need to be complicated or time-consuming. Simple shifts in your communication style, body language, and activity level may be the perfect way to speak love to your child.

Here is a short list of ideas to get you thinking about connecting with your kids:

- Nonverbal: smiling, showing kind eyes, nodding, mirroring their emotion with your face, putting your phone away when you're together

- Empathy: seeing things from your child's perspective, putting emotion words to their experiences, limiting logic and reasoning when your child is experiencing a big emotion

- Body language: speaking to them with open arms, getting on your child's level, turning toward them when they are speaking

- Active listening: asking clarifying questions; resisting the urge to correct, direct, or problem-solve; focusing on hearing their perspective rather than being right or having the last word

- Safe touches: backrubs, hand massages, hugs, carrying/holding, piggyback rides, cuddling

- Play: outdoor games, imagination, creative activities, roughhousing, silliness, singing

- Support: offering comfort, helping with a project, sharing a snack, teaching new skills

When it comes to connection, we want to use our energy and time in a way that truly speaks love to our unique child. Connection will look different for every child, which means it may look different for every child in your home. Rather than forcing your kids to connect the same way, start by noticing how your child responds. Does their face light up when you sit down to cuddle on the couch? Do they seem to open up when you spend extra time during bedtime tuck in? Does a game of tag seem to ease the tension for a while? Is a lunchbox note saved in a special place? Do they seem to need a lot of physical contact, or do they seem to need their space? Are they more active or quieter?

When your child is young, you will need to tune into their cues, learning through observation what types of connection work best for them. As your children grow, you can work together to create the ideal situation for connection. You can ask, "What do I do that makes you feel the most special?" Or, "If we had fifteen minutes together, just the two of us, how would we spend our time?" You may want to get more specific: "When you come home from school, do you need space, or do you want to talk with me about your day?" Or, "How many hugs do you need from me each day?" The more detail you get about the things that make them feel heard, understood, and seen, the more you can add them to your daily routine.

## TWO KINDS OF CONNECTION

Once you start to notice how your child feels connected, you may naturally add it to your life without another thought. It may flow easily into your routine and communication patterns. For other families, connection may seem a little less obvious and may not come naturally. Both responses are normal. If you're struggling to understand how to practically incorporate connection into your life, start by separating it into two categories: proactive connection and in-the-moment connection.

Proactive connection is those actions, activities, and words spoken on a consistent basis. In-the-moment connection is your response during a challenging parenting situation, like a meltdown or a disagreement. Both types of connection are important, and both play a role in helping your child self-regulate, manage their big feelings, and feel secure in their attachment to you and other caregivers.

One of the best ways to incorporate proactive connection is daily one-on-one time. This is a ten- or fifteen-minute block of time you set aside to spend with your child regularly—daily, if possible. The goal for this time is for you and your child to have fun together. It should be free of distractions like checking your phone, making dinner, answering email, or attending to another child. During this block of time, your child chooses an activity to do together. If your child is active, they may want to jump on the trampoline or play tag. If your child is creative, they may want to color. If your child needs a listening ear, they may just want to talk. Your job is to be engaged and present. This is not the time to lecture, correct, or direct the activity.

Having consistent one-on-one time fills their connection "bucket" so to speak. It reassures your child that you have time for them, they are not a burden, and you enjoy spending time together. They feel loved, seen, and valued. When you have a consistent schedule, they know they can rely on you, that you're trustworthy, and that they don't have to compete with siblings or other distractions to have your undivided attention.

The second type of connection is in-the-moment connection. Even with proactive connection time, our kids will still struggle to manage their big feelings, emotions, and stress. This dysregulation may come out as aggression, anxiety, not listening, throwing toys, or fighting with siblings. In these moments, we have a choice—connection or disconnection—as our first response.

The last chapter talked about how a connecting response in tense, emotional situations, can help build a strong, resilient brain. Parenting techniques such as giving timeouts, grounding, taking things away, yelling, or ignoring can cause a disconnection between us and our children. Sometimes, this disconnection is physical, such as sending a child to their room. Other times, it is emotional, such as when we tell our kids to "calm down!" when we are obviously not calm ourselves. Connecting before we correct means we are willing to slow down and be empathetic, and sometimes even playful, to help our children through their big feelings.

In-the-moment connections may also be helpful during times of physical separation like daycare drop-off, coming home after school, bedtime, and getting up from a nap. You may notice an increase in challenging behaviors when you and your child have been separated or will soon separate. Even routine and relatively short separations can be a source of unease and discomfort for some children. Your first reaction may be "I was only at the store for an hour!" But your child's behavior may be telling you "I need to be reminded that I am safe and loved."

We are imperfect parents; we're not going to get this right every time. We're going to struggle with our own triggers, stress, and emotional regulation. This is normal. If you are struggling to self-regulate the majority of the time, it may be time to seek support from a mental health provider. We cannot connect with our kids in a healthy way if we are not as healthy as we can be.

## CONNECTION FOR BUSY FAMILIES

As you read those descriptions, you may feel a sense of panic rise in your chest. You are already so busy, you barely have time to think. How are you supposed to find time to connect with your kids daily—let alone in the middle of a huge meltdown?

Deep breaths.

Busy schedules are often disconnected schedules. Even though you're in the car together, running kids to various sports or activities, the time may not feel like connection to your child. Your family may be so busy, you cannot have dinner or an afternoon outing together. Sometimes scheduling demands are outside of our control or our lives are extremely busy for a season.

There is nothing wrong with being a busy, active family as long as connection is working for your kids. If you feel that your schedule could use a little margin, take some time with your calendar and look for things that could be dropped, rescheduled, changed, or decreased. If your kids are old enough, have a family meeting to discuss your busyness and check in on how everyone is feeling with regards to the pace of the day or week. Prioritize things that bring your family joy and make everyone feel that they belong.

Yes, connection is often done at a slower and more deliberate pace than our busy, hectic lives. Yes, adjusting your schedule, or your mindset, to prioritize connection may take some work initially.

However, connection is one of the most important parenting strategies you can implement. When kids feel connected to their caregivers, they don't have to wonder if they are valued, they don't have to compete with siblings for a place in the family. They can rest, grow, and learn. But sometimes, regardless of your hectic schedule, kids need more reassurance and connection throughout the day.

Miniconnections are short connection "check-ins" to remind your child that they are seen and loved. They only take a few minutes or even a few seconds. This might mean instead of playing a full game of Monopoly, you play a three-minute game of War. Or instead of shooting baskets together, you stand on the sidelines and compliment their improving form. It might mean giving an encouraging shoulder squeeze to your child as they complete a homework assignment or taking a quick break from making dinner to give your full attention as your child tells a story.

If your child seems to be having a difficult day or if the tension seems to be building, it may be a good indication that they need a few extra miniconnections.

Sometimes all your child needs is a quick reminder that you see them in their big feelings. Your goal is not to make these big feelings go away but to be present with them through the difficult times, reassuring them, once again, that they are not alone.

Connection is a dance. Some things will work, some will not, and that's OK. Some of your connection attempts will be met with resistance and some will work out beautifully. You don't need to connect with your kids perfectly to have a strong, respectful, positive relationship with them.

This is not about getting it right 100 percent of the time. It's about learning and growing together. Making mistakes and working to repair them. Give yourself grace during this process.

But what happens if your child resists your attempts at connection? The next chapter will look at the role shame can play in relationships.

## IT STARTS WITH YOU

- What is your favorite way to connect with your kids?

- What is your child/children's favorite way to connect with you?

- If you do not have one-on-one time with each child right now, how can you add intentional connection time to your routine?

CHAPTER 13

# The "Bad Kid" Cycle

**Not every kid wants to be** seen. I can say that with
confidence because I was that kid. And that teenager. And,
unfortunately, that adult. Of course, I didn't have a word for this
when I was young. All I knew was that I should make myself as
small as possible so no one would see my mistakes.

I got pretty good at hiding in plain sight.

It wasn't until recently that I recognized how much of a grip
shame had on my day-to-day existence. Sitting in my therapist's
office, I started piecing together my desire to be seen as a
good person while trying extremely hard to be an even better
person . . . just in case I wasn't.

We cannot talk about connection without talking about
shame. Connection is about knowing, loving, and seeing
another person. Shame is about hiding. While connection sends
the message "You belong," shame sends the message "If they
knew the 'real' you, they would reject you."

The two have a hard time coexisting.

Combating shame with God's grace and unconditional love
has been a slow process of self-compassion and rewriting
my inner dialogue. But I am thankful that I did the work to
understand the power of shame because it has given me a

unique opportunity to see the behavior of my children and other parents in a new way. I am able to see behaviors others write off as "anxiety" or "aggression" as a cover-up for intense feelings of shame.

Maybe you can relate.

Maybe you can trace your experiences of shame back to a specific situation or a specific statement in your childhood. Or maybe, like me, you have always felt this way. Maybe becoming a parent was the catalyst for feelings of shame. Maybe you're only now recognizing the role shame plays in your parenting.

If you struggle with shame, you are not alone. Welcome to the shame community. We will work to overcome these negative thoughts and embrace our true worth together.

## SHAME VERSUS GUILT

Though we may not be able to name it, most parents want their children to have a sense of healthy guilt. We want them to recognize that they did something wrong, feel bad about it, apologize, make amends, and move forward in a positive direction. Let's imagine your kids are building block towers next to each other on the floor. Your older son feels jealous that his brother's tower looks cooler than his. As his feeling of jealousy builds, he reaches out and knocks over his brother's tower.

The inner dialogue of a child responding with healthy guilt would sound something like "Oh no, that was a mistake! I feel bad about my decision. It's wrong to knock over someone else's blocks." With your help, he might say, "I'm sorry I knocked over your tower. Can I help you rebuild it?"

Unhealthy guilt is disproportionate, irrational, misplaced. You may feel guilty about something someone else did or said, even if you were not involved. Going back to the block towers, let's imagine your older son accidentally knocks over his sibling's block tower. Then for the rest of the afternoon, he apologizes profusely, repeating, "I'm so sorry I knocked over your tower," even though it was unintentional and his brother has long moved past the incident.

Shame is an internal dialogue that focuses the light on you as the problem. In either situation—knocking the blocks down because of jealousy or knocking down the blocks accidentally—the inner dialogue will be the same: "You are a mistake. You are a failure." If a parent attempts to redirect, correct, or even empathize with the child's emotions, their alarm may sound, leading to aggressive behavior. They may run away. They may point the finger or blame others. They may slump their shoulders and avoid eye contact. The inner dialogue continues: "Don't let anyone see the real you. They will reject you. You are unlovable."

## THE "BAD KID" CYCLE

This may seem like an extreme reaction to a crumbling block tower. Unfortunately, for many people struggling to combat shame, this is an everyday conversation. Some kids battling with these shame-filled thoughts get stuck in what I call, the "bad kid" cycle.

To understand this cycle, we need to slow things down and look deeper into the inner dialogue of shame. Without language to explain this cycle, most kids (and parents) feel confused and overwhelmed. Some don't even realize there's a cycle. And even if they recognize it, they feel stuck, unsure how to find a way out.

The example that follows shows one way a child may get stuck in the "bad kid" cycle.

A child acts in a way that leads to unpleasant consequences. This might be an accident, like dropping a bottle of orange juice. Or it might be fueled by a big emotion, like ripping up a difficult homework assignment. Or it might be something that is beyond their developmental stage, like letting go of a balloon string outside. For many kids, if a caring adult connects with them in this moment, a sense of healthy guilt will kick in; they will clean up, apologize, and move on with their day.

However, if the parent yells, punishes, overreacts, or reprimands the child for their behavior on a consistent basis, the child may head into a shame spiral. Instead of seeing their actions as a mistake, an accident, or a normal part of learning and growing, the shame starts speaking—a small voice inside says, "You are a mistake. You are a failure."

This message feels extremely yucky inside. No one likes to hear this about themselves. At first, the voice may be nothing more than a whisper. It may be easy to quiet the voice and push the uncomfortable feeling to the side. But when a child hears this message repeatedly or does not have strategies to combat it, the voice grows. The volume is louder and the feeling more intense. The message is "You are unlovable." Listening to this voice can be an alarm trigger. It may send the child into a fight, flight, or freeze behavior: yelling, complaining, blaming, pointing the finger, hitting, throwing things, running away, or avoiding eye contact.

Being in an "alarm" state can be scary and overwhelming. And for some children becoming aggressive only intensifies the inner shame message: "Wow. Look at you now! You're really out of control. See, you really are a failure." They may try to ignore these horrible feelings and deny their actions so they appear lovable, contradicting the obvious by saying, "I didn't hit my sister" or "I'm not angry." It doesn't seem logical from an outside perspective, but at this moment, your child is dysregulated. They are not thinking clearly; they are simply responding to the perceived threat of losing connection with their caregiver.

When a parent observes these behaviors, the first instinct is to react. You don't know that shame is fueling these behaviors; all you see is the aggression. All you hear are excuses and denial. And in the heat of the moment, it seems that these actions need to be addressed. You may say something like "It's not OK to hit!" or "Come back here and clean up this mess!" When your child doesn't calm down or take responsibility for their actions, your own alarm begins to blare. This leads to yelling or overreacting. Some parents send the child into time-out, punish, or give a consequence.

Unfortunately, this reaction reinforces the child's inner dialogue: "See, you're a failure. Even your parents think so. You are a bad kid." The more often this pattern repeats, the easier it is for the child to internalize the voice of shame—now it's how the child sees themselves: "I'm a bad kid."

Like the neurons firing and wiring together, the more often she tells herself "I'm a bad kid," the more she believes it. And the more she believes it, the more often her behavior reflects it. Her brain is on high alert. Since she believes she is a bad kid, her actions often align with her inner dialogue. Blame and aggression may become her first response to correction. And yet she may also know that these behaviors are wrong and wish she could stop, but she doesn't know how. Some kids become vigilantly committed to never making a mistake or being seen as lacking in any way. Of course, this is impossible, but when shame tells you you're unlovable if you make a mistake, perfection seems to be the only way to ensure connection.

Making things even more complicated, once this pattern is in place, even an empathetic or connecting response from a caregiver may be met with resistance. Recognizing your child is struggling, you decide to offer a hug, only to be pushed away, verbally or physically. Naming a feeling with empathy ensures a quick denial. Their reaction is confusing and frustrating. You're not sure how to act or what would help. If you knew the child's inner dialogue, it may sound like "Get away from me! Can't you see I messed up? I'm a bad kid. I don't deserve love."

Without insight into the role of shame in the behavior, the parent may decide that what the child needs is more discipline or a stricter punishment, reinforcing the message and keeping the child stuck.

Shame is the powerful force that keeps this cycle spinning.

Not every child will find themselves in the "bad kid cycle." Some children embrace mistakes without a second thought, never letting these failures define who they are. And not every child who struggles with shame will look, sound, or act the same. The goal is to notice. To be curious about your unique child's behaviors. To recognize that there may be more going on than meets the eye. And to be aware of the sneaky way shame can impact your child's actions. Your child is not destined to be in the "bad kid cycle" forever. We will talk about breaking free from this cycle in the next chapter. Until then, know that your commitment to connection is a force more powerful than shame will ever be.

## REWRITING YOUR SHAME STORY

Reading this may send you into your own "bad parent" cycle. You may recognize yourself in the parent's response. Or you may recognize yourself in the child's perspective. You may suddenly realize your child is stuck in the "bad kid" cycle. Or you may realize that you've been in it since you were a child.

If your inner dialogue is telling you that you are a failure, that you are unlovable, or that you should hide your failures so no one will realize that you are imperfect—congratulations! You've recognized and named shame. You're one step closer to removing it from your life.

The story you tell yourself in this moment is important. You can either continue to listen to the lies that shame wants you to believe or rewrite the narrative. Neither path is easy. Breaking through shame is difficult work, but it can be done. In fact, the best way to help your child escape this cycle is by breaking through the shame in your own life. So if you're ready, take a deep breath. Listen to your own inner dialogue. Notice the tone of voice you use with yourself; notice the choice of words. Pay attention to your defensiveness. Notice if your inner voice says, "Yeah, but remember all these failures . . ." Or if "shoulds" fill your mind: "You should have known about shame before now." "You shouldn't have yelled so much." "You should be able to manage their big feelings by now." If you've been gripped by shame for a long time, these voices may sound familiar.

Remember, we are all imperfect. We all make mistakes. Work to make a distinction between shame, unhealthy guilt, and healthy guilt. Shame tells you, "You are unlovable. Don't let anyone see your mistakes." Unhealthy guilt says, "This is all your fault." Healthy guilt makes space for learning and growing in a positive direction. It says, "I overreacted and yelled. That was a mistake. I will practice taking a deep breath before I react next time."

Then with the support of friends, a coparent, or a mental health provider, commit to changing the language you use to describe yourself, your worth, and your ability to receive love. Refocus your attention on grace. Make room for forgiveness—especially forgiving yourself.

Shame wants to hide.

It cannot exist when we are vulnerable. When we name it. When we open ourselves up to connection in a safe community.

Your child doesn't need to stay stuck in the "bad kid" cycle. And you are not stuck in the "bad parent" cycle. The next chapter will talk about breaking through shame and breaking this cycle.

## IT STARTS WITH YOU

- Which do you struggle with more: shame or unhealthy guilt?

- Can you identify your child on the "bad kid" cycle?

- Are you stuck in a shame spiral after reading this chapter? Who can you reach out to for support?

# CHAPTER 14

# How to Combat Shame

**I heard the crash before I** saw what happened. There was panic in the air. The silence spoke volumes: my kids were afraid of my reaction.

Stepping into the room, I had a choice—overreact or take a deep breath.

"What happened?" I asked cautiously.

Following their eyes, I saw the broken teapot. And though it was the set from my childhood, it wasn't irreplaceable.

"Oh, the teapot handle. Let's see if a little glue will fix it."

Relief filled the room as we gathered the pieces.

I wasn't always aware of the impact this one moment could have on my kids. Children can feel shame as early as eighteen months (guilt comes later, between three and six years old), so by the time I started recognizing shame in my own life, my daughter was already trapped in the "bad kid" cycle. I didn't use time-outs or punishments with her when she was young, but my words and actions still impacted her internal dialogue.

Once I identified shame, things changed.

My responses became softer. I saw her anxiety and aggression differently. I saw my own shame playing a role in our back-and-forth conversations. I started from a grace-first perspective rather than a behavior-first perspective.

With time and patience, we are interrupting the "bad kid" cycle one big feeling at a time.

I am excited for my daughter. She has words for the internal dialogue. She is empowered with strategies and skills that can be practiced for years to come.

And it starts with connection.

## COMBATING SHAME

Shame is a force. Once the pattern is wired into a person's brain, it's not easily rewired. When you think about helping your child through shame, I'd encourage you to see this as a long-term goal. The process will take time, patience, and a lot of love. This is not going to be an overnight success. It may take longer than you'd like. It's OK if you feel frustrated or sad as you watch and wait for your child to find their way out of the "bad kid" cycle.

Your response is the most important key to helping your child combat shame. Your goal is to help your child feel seen, loved, appreciated, included, and respected. Regardless of their behavior. I will say that again. Your calm, confident response is necessary, even if your child is yelling, hitting, avoiding, or noncompliant. I know this is challenging. It may feel like "giving in" or "being too soft." It may even feel impossible at times. That is OK. You do not need to be a robot parent. You can still have your own emotions, and you can process them with another adult or mental health professional. But in the heat of the moment, we want to send the message "I see you and I love you. Yes, even now. Yes, even when you are acting like this or saying those things. You are loved."

We cannot send this message if our alarm is blaring. Your brain is going to send the message "Threat! This behavior needs to be stopped immediately!" Those messages aren't helpful. We need to stay in our thinking brain so we can be empathetic, creative, and confident. We need to use every connection method to make sure our children get the message "You are loved." This means you can use your body language—arms open, sitting down, staying present—to show love. You can use empathy to let them know you feel their pain. You can use physical touch—like a soft pat on the back or a hand massage—to offer comfort, even if they initially move away. Your response is all about seeing past the defenses to the underlying pain. To the shame. To the messages that say they are unlovable.

Keep the statement "neurons that fire together, wire together" in mind. Each and every time you respond with connection, you wire a few neurons. Individual interactions may not seem to be making a difference, but the change is happening on a cellular level. Think of it as paving a new road through a mountain. It's going to take time to chip through, level it out, and smooth it down before it's ready for a new message to speed through. Deep breaths. Your child needs you to stay calm and confident, especially when they do not feel either of those emotions.

We want our children to feel loved, known, and seen. And we know that children who feel shame often do not want to be seen.

Or at least that's what their internal dialogue tells them.

## TEACHING YOUR CHILD ABOUT SHAME

Shame cannot stand being named. It wants to stay hidden and unknown. When we start pulling shame into the light, it loses its power. It's a vulnerable step, but it's essential to helping your child combat shame.

Start by putting words around the experience of shame with your child. Say the word "shame" out loud. Write it down or draw a picture. Talk about how sneaky shame can be and how it sends messages that only our brain can hear. If your child is old enough, see if they can identify any of these messages. Talk about how shame feels in a body. Often, shame wants us to slump our shoulders, turn our eyes down or away from others; sometimes we actually move away from others or activities. Sometimes, shame feels hot, angry, and intense. Muscles can tense, fists may clench, and your body may be prepared for a fight. Remind your child that shame doesn't want to be seen—so pushing people away from you with aggression is a totally natural response! Other people may feel a stomachache or headache. They may feel like a task, project, or request needs to be completed perfectly in order to be acceptable because shame lies to us by saying we can't be loved just for who we are or what we (imperfectly) do. Even though these are lies told by that sneaky internal voice, the actions they produce follow along a very logical path.

The next step to combating shame is addressing that sneaky, lying internal dialogue. We can help our children learn self-compassionate phrases to use when they are stuck in the "bad kid" cycle. Compassion means giving yourself kindness rather than criticism in a situation that is painful or difficult. Kristin Neff, a self-compassion researcher, suggests talking to yourself how you would talk to a close friend who is going through the same challenges.[1] For example, "If Tessa was having trouble with a math problem, what would you say to her?" or "If Lincoln had a disagreement with his brother, how would you help him make it right?" These conversations may not come easily to your child, and that is OK. If your child is young or struggles with this step, you may have to be this self-compassionate voice until they internalize it for themselves. Remember, this is a slow process. Introducing compassion to a person stuck in a shame cycle can feel like learning a foreign language; it takes practice.

Once you've set the foundation, by naming shame and practicing self-compassion, you can help your child change the story about the role shame plays in their life. In the past, the story may have been "Oh no! I made a mistake! Don't tell mom; she'll be mad. Pretend that everything is fine." Now you can help them rewrite the narrative: "Oh no, I made a mistake. Everyone makes mistakes. Mom loves me and will not stop loving me. Sharing this with her does not make me a bad kid." If your child's story used to be "Big feelings need to be avoided at all costs. When I get mad, I can't stop. I'll stay mad forever. Big feelings are overwhelming and bad, and my parents don't like me when I'm angry," you can help them change the language: "Everyone feels big feelings. Big feelings come and go. Even though I feel mad now, I know how to get my brain back to calm again. I'm not alone; my parents are there to support me. They love me when I'm happy and they love me when I'm mad. My feelings don't change their love for me. My feelings don't make me a bad kid."

Rewriting the story will look different depending on your child's age and developmental stage. When your child is young, you will need to make some educated guesses about your child's internal dialogue, and tell their story out loud in your own words. Use simple words and encouraging phrases that your child can repeat to themselves as they grow: "Samuel is loved no matter what. Mom and Dad will always love me. Samuel will always belong in our family. Samuel will make mistakes and Mom and Dad will still love him." As your child grows and learns more about naming shame's internal messages, you can work together to create a new narrative. Sometimes, even if your child is old enough to talk about shame, they may need you to remind them of their new story. They may rely on you to rewrite the story—perhaps for the hundredth time—until they are able to fully embrace it as their own.

Changing the story about your worth is not easy. Strategies like empathy, calming, and connection may not seem to "work" in the moment because your child may be slow to change their behavior. Your child may be hesitant to believe the new story. They may physically or verbally resist being comforted. Children who are stuck in shame are often resistant to believing anything other than the shame-filled messages. As damaging as these messages are, they are the ones that are familiar. Accepting a different reality, even one provided by a caregiver, takes courage.

You may feel frustrated during this process. It's normal to feel discouraged when your child seems to be stuck in an uncomfortable emotion or unhealthy view of themselves. It's OK if these conversations are awkward and clumsy at first. It may take time to feel confident talking about shame and creating a new story. Empowering kids to know, understand, and identify shame in their lives gives them the power to overcome it, but it is not a one-time conversation. It's something you and your child can talk about over time, slowly learning to identify when shame shows up, how it feels, the words it says, and the way it presents itself to the outside world.

Not every family can work through shame on their own. If your child seems especially stuck in shame, or if you struggle to know how to walk through these steps with your child, it may be time to seek the support of a mental health professional. You do not need to do this on your own. Seeking support may be the best way to educate yourself and your child about shame and learn how to rewrite the story together.

Be proud of yourself for offering an alternative to shame, and be proud of your child anytime they take even the smallest step toward seeing a different vision of themselves: as lovable no matter what.

## A WORK IN PROGRESS

You have an amazing opportunity to support your child as they combat shame. Rather than beating yourself up for not noticing shame or for using disconnecting parenting strategies in the past, see this as your first step in the right direction.

You may not have known about connection or shame before today. And now you do.

You may not have known how to help your child. And now you have a place to start.

This is something not to be criticized but celebrated!

Going forward, you're not going to do this perfectly. Remember, it's not about perfection. Ever. Parenting is a process of constantly learning, growing, and making changes to benefit our children. We're going to get it wrong sometimes. We're going to get it right sometimes. Your kids don't need perfect parents, no matter what your inner shame dialogue tells you.

The steps above are not just for your kids. They're also steps you can take to combat shame in your own life. Where do you need to start? Maybe you need to be aware of the negative messages shame is telling you. Maybe you need to notice how you talk to yourself throughout the day.

Maybe you need to practice self-compassion, rewriting your inner dialogue in a way that is kind and compassionate, the way you would talk to a close friend. Or, maybe it's time to rewrite the whole story. To remind yourself that you are loved, valuable, and worthy just because you're you! That there isn't an expectation of perfection or a requirement that you stay neutral and unemotional; that it is OK to have feelings and to express them to others.

Maybe it's time to come out of hiding. To find the connection you need in community with others. Maybe you need to share your parenting challenges with a group of caring parents in your community or reach out for support from a mental health professional. Maybe you need to be honest about your struggles and find that you are not alone, that even if others experience different challenges, they can relate because parenting is hard, and none of us are doing it perfectly.

Don't let your own shame message keep you stuck!

Every parenting strategy in this book is meant to be connecting and shame-combating. As you learn more, you can feel confident that each step along the way will help you see, know, and love your children—and yourself—well.

Sometimes, connection will seem easy and your relationship will be strong and healthy. Let's look at what to do when connection seems challenging.

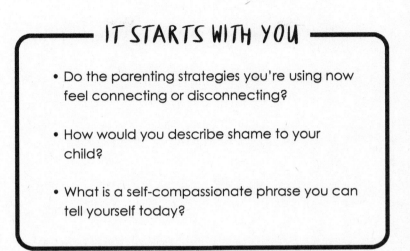

## IT STARTS WITH YOU

- Do the parenting strategies you're using now feel connecting or disconnecting?

- How would you describe shame to your child?

- What is a self-compassionate phrase you can tell yourself today?

# CHAPTER 15

# Troubleshooting Connection

**I am a morning person.** Not in the sense that I'm chipper and energetic at 5:30 a.m. More in the fact that I enjoy getting up before my family and soaking in the quiet calm before the storm. I know, as I'm sitting in my favorite chair, that in a matter of minutes, my kids will be waking up, wanting to tell me about their dreams, needing to cuddle, and asking for help getting breakfast.

If I'm honest, there are mornings when I dread the sound of their cute little footsteps coming down the hall.

My desire for alone time, my love of reading, my personal space, all take a back seat to the needs of my children in the morning.

This is parenting. I wouldn't change it. And sometimes, I struggle to find the energy to connect with my kids in a meaningful way. Especially in the morning when I'm enjoying a cup of tea and a good book. Alone.

I say this because I don't want you to get the impression that connecting with our kids is always joyful. It's OK if you have mixed feelings about it. You are still a human, with needs and likes and dislikes, just as your children are. There will be times when you look at your children and feel like you could burst with delight, and other times when it will be difficult to focus on how amazing they are because a work deadline looms, you didn't sleep well last night, or the dog just threw up on the carpet.

Not every parent is a carefree, game-playing parent. Not every parent loves cuddling up and sharing a book with their child. Not every parent enjoys alone time. You don't have to master a video game or learn how to skateboard to connect with your child. It's OK if you don't love playing with LEGOs or if messy play makes you cringe. You have a unique personality that is going to make connecting with your kids a unique experience. Instead of thinking that you "should" connect in a particular way or comparing yourself to other families, focus on what works for you and your kids.

Remember, connection is more than sharing an ice cream cone or watching funny cat videos together. It's about making your kids feel seen, known, and loved. It's an attitude. A relationship. When I set my book aside and pull my child into my lap, I'm connecting. Small intentions like smiles, hugs, and encouraging notes all count!

If the thought of connecting with your kids makes you feel exhausted or you simply do not have anything to give another human being, it's time to focus on yourself. This is not a selfish step; it's the most important step. When you are feeling depleted, it's a warning sign that something in your life needs attention. Sometimes we are not able to make dramatic changes to our life circumstances. Sometimes it's simply a difficult stage of life that will eventually pass. Other times, though, there are concrete steps you can take to refill your bucket so you have energy and attention to give your children.

Take a deep breath and examine your current life situation. What things are making you feel overwhelmed? What tasks seem like too much right now? How is your eating? Your sleep? Your exercise? What types of support do you need? Who can you ask for help? Where do you find community? Who can you reach out to for connection?

Seeking help and support from others is a difficult first step. Shame can make us want to hide our flaws and imperfections. Shame can tell us we "shouldn't need help" in the first place. Those messages are lies. We were created for connection. You deserve—and need—connection as much as your children do. You are worthy of healthy, encouraging connections in your life.

## WHEN KIDS DON'T WANT TO CONNECT

Sometimes, our attempts to connect with our kids don't go as planned. Instead of melting into our arms, our kids physically push back. Instead of cheerfully joining in a game, they complain. When we offer empathy, they reply, "You don't know how I feel!" These reactions sting. Especially when we're going out of our way to do something nice or getting out of our comfort zone to strengthen the relationship.

If you notice a disconnect in your connection, start by examining your own triggers. Think to yourself, "Why does their reaction bother me so much?" or "What is it about their response that brings up a negative response in my body?" Sit with your responses for a while rather than pushing them aside. Maybe you'll find that you miss the snuggly toddler years or that connecting with a tween is more difficult than you expected. Maybe you'll realize that their reaction hurts your feelings or makes you feel like you're failing. You may decide to talk about your triggers with a trusted friend, hear their stories, and recognize that you are not alone. Explore what you need to be able to stay calm and confident, even if your kids are struggling to regulate their emotions.

After thinking about your reactions, think about your method of connection. Ask yourself if this is a connection strategy that worked in the past or that your child seems to enjoy. If not, you may try something else. If your child is old enough, you may decide to open up the conversation with them, saying something like "I've noticed you pull away when I try to hug you. What's up?" Brainstorm other ways of connection with one another. But keep in mind, everyone has bad days. Sometimes, even a connection attempt that "worked" in the past will not "work" in the future, simply because your child is having an off day.

If you're being more intentional about your connection attempts, your child may be skeptical of your behavior at first. They may wonder if your request to play soccer in the yard will end up in a lecture about good sportsmanship. They may worry that sitting together to work on homework is just your way of keeping their grades in check. Being consistent is important. Make sure connections are truly a time for relationship building, saving correction and direction for another time. With time, your child will come to trust your intentions, seeing these attempts not as manipulation but as being truly seen and known by you.

Shame, guilt, and trauma can all impact how our children connect with us. Remember that when a brain is in fight or flight mode, the thinking brain shuts down. Everything, even calm connection, can be seen as a threat, often causing a child to act aggressively or shut down. Their response isn't necessarily a reflection on your actions; it's a biological response. Giving your child space when the brain is in the alarm state may encourage them to connect with you again once they are back to calm. If your child is repeatedly resistant to connection attempts, even in calm moments, it may be helpful to reach out to a mental health professional for additional support.

It's easy to feel like giving up when connection attempts seem to be ineffective. As our kids grow, our old ways of connection may not be as effective as they were when they were younger. Don't give up! We never outgrow our need to belong. Rather than trying the same things, look for other ways to connect. Send an encouraging text, share a funny meme, or watch silly YouTube videos. Hide notes in their room or backpack. Simply smile when they come into the room. And maybe one of the most effective, resist the urge to use every conversation as an opportunity to criticize, correct, or teach. Instead, challenge yourself to find the positive, pointing out things they're doing well, even if they seem small or inconsequential.

A healthy, positive connection starts with you. Your willingness and attempts at connection should not depend on your child's response. Presenting a calm, confident, connecting attitude is the goal. Connection with your child should not be contingent on your child's good behavior or welcoming response. It should not be doled out in measured amounts, only when your child is calm and happy. True connection means you're willing to "see" your children as they are, the good, the challenging, and everything in between.

Of course, we will never do this perfectly. Catching ourselves when we pull away or feel resistant to connecting is a good indicator that our needs are not being met. Addressing our own feelings of depletion, stress, or feelings of overwhelm can help us stay calm and confident, even when our kids are resistant.

## IS CONNECTION CODDLING?

Allowing your child to feel big feelings and offering connection before correction is not an easy shift for some parents. If you're feeling uneasy about this response, you're normal. Even if you're on board with positive parenting and prioritizing connection, you may get feedback from family members or friends that you're being "too soft" or letting your kids get away with behavior, or that the only way to teach them is by giving a consequence.

Connection is a basic need of every human being. Creating an atmosphere of connection is not something that should be earned or based on good behavior. Creating safety and setting reasonable, developmentally appropriate boundaries is also an important part of parenting. Thankfully, these two things can coexist without conflict.

When we respond to our kids with connection, we have two goals. One, we want to remind our kids that they are seen, loved, and valued. We want our kids to know that even in their most challenging moments, we are still present and they still belong. Two, we have an opportunity to support them as they learn self-regulation. Responding in a calm, connected manner builds strong brain connections. Each time we interact in a connecting way, our kids learn that big feelings and difficult situations can be managed—either with the help of a caregiver or with skills they've learned from a supportive caregiver in the past.

Connection is only one step in healthy, positive parenting. Responding with connection first doesn't mean your child can skip their homework or can hit their sister whenever they are angry. Many traditional parenting strategies prioritize teaching right and wrong, using consequences and punishments to reinforce these lessons. Grace-based parenting says, "We'll get to the teaching once your brain is calm and you feel connected enough to listen and learn." It's not letting a child off the hook; it's prioritizing the relationship over rules.

Chances are, you're doing an amazing job teaching right from wrong. If you were to ask your kids, they would probably tell you hurting someone, stealing, and lying are all wrong. They would probably be able to tell you how these behaviors impact others and why they are not good decisions. Even children who know right from wrong struggle to control their behaviors and reactions in the heat of the moment. As immature children with growing self-regulation skills, they are going to make "wrong" choices when they go into fight or flight mode. This is not an excuse; it's a function of brain development and biology. Connection-first parenting acknowledges this as a work in progress rather than something your child should have "figured out by now."

If you're concerned about coddling your kids, it may be beneficial to take a minute to sit with this for a while. What are your fears about connecting? What are your fears about coddling? How were you raised, and how does that compare with how you're parenting now? What do others say about your parenting? How do these things impact you? Sitting with the answers may help you clarify your parenting goals. Maybe you'll find that your fears are totally based on other people's opinions. Or maybe you'll realize that you're really good at connection. Or maybe you'll discover that connection comes easy for you but setting limits is more challenging. Whatever the case, be kind to yourself.

Grace-based parenting can feel very permissive at first. Especially if you grew up in a home with authoritarian parents or a culture where children were not valued as individuals. It's OK if you struggle to figure out how to mesh this new information with your upbringing or understanding of parenting to this point. It may take some time to feel comfortable offering connection when your child is upset or showing a challenging behavior.

Let yourself wrestle with this tension. Give it a try before you decide that it "doesn't work." Reach out to other positive parents for support in the meantime. And remember, there's more to parenting than connection, but if you're going to focus on anything, making your kids feel seen, heard, valued, and loved will never be a waste of time or energy.

Now that we know ourselves and know how to be with our kids in their big feelings, let's explore how to communicate in a way that keeps the relationship strong and connected.

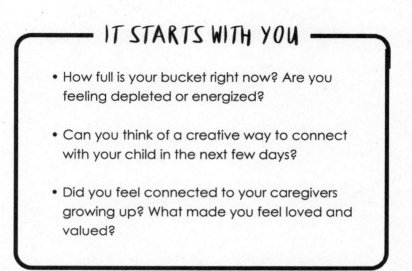

## IT STARTS WITH YOU

- How full is your bucket right now? Are you feeling depleted or energized?

- Can you think of a creative way to connect with your child in the next few days?

- Did you feel connected to your caregivers growing up? What made you feel loved and valued?

CHAPTER 16

# Listening Well

**In preschool classrooms everywhere,** teachers are asking
their three- and four-year-old students to "find their listening
ears." This cue is supposed to remind the children to close their
mouths, turn their eyes to the speaker, and pay attention to
what's being taught.

Unfortunately, this lasts about five seconds before someone
blurts out that their "Papa has a pet bunny," and all the other
children want to know more about the rabbit than what the
teacher is trying to explain.

Adults are not much better than preschoolers when it comes
to listening well.

We may try to concentrate on what our children are telling
us, but within seconds, we're formulating a response, creating
the perfect solution, or cultivating a witty comeback.

I'm guilty of this regularly. Two siblings are fighting in the
other room, and instead of saying, "How can I help?" I come
in yelling, "That's enough!" My daughter has a difficult class
assignment, and instead of listening to her complaints, I ask,
"Have you emailed the teacher?" Someone's feelings were
hurt on the playground, and instead of understanding what
happened and offering comfort, I'm telling her how to respond
next time.

It happens in the blink of an eye.

Just like many of us weren't raised in homes that valued emotional intelligence, we also didn't have a comprehensive education around healthy communication. We're used to defending our positions, fighting to have our voices heard, or stifling our responses because speaking up is unsafe. We may be used to being minimized, ignored, talked over, or dictated to. We may be unclear how to put our thoughts into words, how to set a boundary with kindness, or how to sit with someone else's pain. Maybe we haven't experienced many people listening to us and have very little experience using our "listening ears" with our children.

If this seems new and overwhelming, you're not alone.

Take a deep breath. You don't need to be an expert at this immediately. It's a learning process. It's OK for healthy communication to take time before it becomes second nature. And if you feel completely overwhelmed or if thinking about communication uncovers challenges from your history or your family of origin, please seek support from a mental health professional.

## HEALTHY COMMUNICATION STARTS WITH LISTENING WELL

Creating healthy communication habits in your home may seem like an enormous undertaking, especially if your children are already old enough to talk, yell, scream, use disrespectful language, or ignore you completely. I often hear parents complain, "If they would just listen the first time, then I wouldn't have to yell!" On the surface, that makes a certain kind of sense. Of course our house would be much calmer if everyone complied immediately. Unfortunately, we cannot expect our children to have more maturity, better communication skills, and complex problem-solving strategies if we aren't modeling them first. And besides, as much as you want to raise a child who is compliant, you also want a child who speaks up for the underdog, who fights for what's right, and who knows how to navigate complex conversations.

So rather than expecting our kids to behave better, the focus needs to start with listening well. This means putting your own agenda aside to focus on what the other person is trying to say. In the simplest terms, listening means—stop talking, give the person your attention, and be ready to learn.

The first step may be the most difficult. Stop talking. Literally. We cannot listen well if we are talking, solving the problem, or reprimanding. We need to create space, quiet, where our kids can have an opportunity to share their thoughts, feelings, frustrations, and worries without interruption. Unfortunately, these big feelings often trigger the alarm state in our brains. The adrenaline flows, and we either prepare for a fight, scan for threats, or try to stop the communication immediately. The fight part of you may respond with, "That's not how we talk to each other, young man!" Or the flight part of you may say, "I will not stay here and listen to you if you're going to complain." You may jump into problem-solving mode, with an overwhelming desire to ease your child's pain or rescue them from an uncomfortable emotion.

All these reactions are normal. As parents, we want to save our children from heartache if at all possible. We want our kids to communicate with respect. The problem is, by responding from an alarm state, we are usually talking, not listening. Your child needs your guidance and support. Eventually. But first, let's make sure they feel heard and understood.

Setting healthy boundaries around communication is important. You do not deserve to be spoken to in an abusive manner, and you may need to step in if your kids are speaking disrespectfully to one another. But it's also important to remember that your kids have limited vocabulary to explain their complex feelings and limited opportunities to speak freely about their points of view. If your child says, "I hate broccoli!" The word "hate" may trigger you, and your instinct may be to reprimand your child for using strong language. Listening well means we may need to set our initial reactions aside so we can hear what's actually being expressed: "I'm unhappy that you're serving broccoli. Of all the vegetables, this is my least favorite. 'Hate' is the best word I could find to express my extreme dislike." In a calm moment, after the dust settles, you can help your child build their vocabulary and talk about alternative ways to express their frustrations.

Assumptions about parents, kids, communication, and roles can also impact our ability to listen well. These assumptions may be passed down through generations or spoken out loud; they may even be subconscious. Common examples of assumptions include

- Kids shouldn't talk to their parents like that.

- I need to have the last word because I'm an adult.

- I'm the boss.

- My child won't learn unless I tell him right from wrong.

- Disrespectful kids are bad kids.

- I have to solve this problem immediately.

- He's too young (or immature) to figure this out on his own.

- This is no big deal.

- She doesn't listen to me, so I'm not going to listen to her.

- Kids should not express disappointment or frustration about my decisions.

If you're unclear if assumptions are impacting your listening skills, notice your inner dialogue as your child talks. What do you feel compelled to say or do? What phrases come to mind? What emotion do you feel in your body? Take a deep breath and see if you can name the assumption that is driving the emotion.

When these assumptions show up, listening often goes out the window. We're no longer focused on hearing our child's perspective; instead, we have our own agenda. Even if it's technically good—like offering a solution—the conversation has shifted. It's no longer about our child; it's about us—our words, thoughts, and advice. In these moments, we often switch to logic and reasoning. Thinking that if our children could just see how illogical they are acting, they would change their ways. When that doesn't work, many parents resort to imposing a punishment or consequence, hoping a negative experience would eliminate big feelings and put an end to a difficult or uncomfortable conversation. Of course, these responses often lead to more yelling, disagreements, and disconnection rather than solutions and peace.

Being quiet is difficult, and it is key to listening well. If your tendency is to talk a lot, if you're a problem-solver, if you're quick to anger, or if one of these assumptions is driving your response, it's time to pause. Take a deep breath. Use this moment to explore why making space for silence is challenging. Go back to the earlier sections in this book and work through the questions or create a calming plan. Calm brains make good choices. And calm brains make great listeners.

If you or your child are stuck in an unproductive conversation, it's OK to take a break. You may need to say, "I want to listen to you, but I am feeling overwhelmed and need a few minutes for my brain to calm down." Or, "We cannot have a good conversation when we are both yelling. Let's take a ten-minute break and try again." Or you may say, "This conversation is getting too heated right now. Would you like help to calm down so we can continue?" Your child may refuse to take these breaks, but that doesn't mean you need to continue to engage. Take responsibility for yourself, and do what you need to do to calm your brain and body and return to the conversation.

As you practice healthy communication with your kids, you may find yourself falling into old habits, especially when things are stressful or overwhelming. This is normal! Rather than beating yourself up about making a mistake, focus on noticing. Notice how you feel when your child expresses a big feeling. Notice how you feel when your child wants your full attention. Notice when you interrupt and which words and phrases you use regularly. Notice if you tend to minimize a situation, make it bigger, want it to go away, or try to solve it. The more you know about your communication style under stress, the easier it will be to spot unhealthy patterns when they pop up, and the better you will be at choosing to be a calm listener.

## LISTENING WELL IS NOT EASY

Sometimes it's uncomfortable to listen. The things you hear are harsh and rude, raw, and illogical. It may feel counterintuitive to allow a child to speak without correcting. Healthy communication doesn't excuse these behaviors, but it also doesn't quiet them just to keep the peace. For some kids, sharing their real and unpleasant feelings is the path to feeling known and moving forward. Naming their feelings, even the unpleasant ones, often decreases the intensity of those feelings, allowing the child to take a deep breath and calm their nervous system. Listening to intense emotions sends the message "I love all parts of you, even the ones that are big and loud."

As the parent of a nonstop talker, I know the exhaustion that comes from needing to give your all to a child as they explain each step of their day in excruciating detail. Or, listening to a child explain their favorite video game or playing card collection. No one can say you don't listen enough. For nonstop talkers, listening to the small and mundane things is a way to build connection. It's a way to say, "I care about you and the things that are important to you." It's also OK to set limits around your availability. Schedule consistent one-on-one time with your child, making sure to build in plenty of time for their detailed stories. If you're feeling pulled in a million directions, you may need to say, "I want to listen, but I can't give you my full attention right now. When I finish this task, I'll meet you at the table to hear more about your day." Then follow through, giving them your listening ear.

I'm also a parent to an "I don't know" child. A child who, no matter how bad they are feeling inside, cannot find the words to express their inner thoughts. A whole different type of exhaustion comes from trying to listen to kids who are speechless. It's challenging to sit with their not-knowing when all you want to do is understand their pain. It's difficult not to put words to their experience or push it aside: "Well, if you can't tell me what's wrong, I'm going to the other room." Sitting and listening to the silence in these moments sends the message "You don't have to have it all figured out to be comforted. I love you even in the not-knowing." Some "I don't know" kids truly need help processing and expressing their feelings and thoughts. Some just need more time before they're ready or able to share. Experiment with the best way to support your child when they're uncertain, overwhelmed, or confused by their inner thoughts and feelings.

Sometimes a child's silence is concerning. You may be more than willing to offer a listening ear when they are struggling, but they resist or pull away. Sometimes this is a sign that your child needs more help managing their big feelings and getting to a place where they feel safe enough to share them with you. If your child expresses an immediate desire to hurt themselves or others, shares something concerning, seems uncharacteristically quiet, or isolates from social situations they previously enjoyed, you should seek support from a mental health professional.

Learning to listen well may stir up all sorts of emotions inside. You may grieve the fact that you were never listened to as a child or that you do not feel heard in your current relationships. You may feel uncertain about your role. You may recognize that listening is really challenging for you, or you may feel that you haven't been a good listener to your kids lately. Whatever you're feeling right now is normal.

Remember, you do not need to be a superhuman listener. You can be an imperfect parent, choosing to push aside the instinct to solve, minimize, or teach and focusing on making sure you hear what your child is saying before you respond.

Give yourself grace as you learn to interrupt old habits and introduce new, respectful communication skills to your family.

After listening, you may be ready to launch into a lengthy lecture; unfortunately, we're not ready for that step yet. Instead, let's learn how to add empathy to our conversations.

## IT STARTS WITH YOU

- How did your family communicate when you were growing up?

- What assumptions do you hold about kids expressing their thoughts and feelings?

- Will being quiet be easy or difficult for you?

# CHAPTER 17

# Being Empathetic

**My kids have numerous health** complaints every day. Anything from small scrapes and bumps to headaches and stomachaches. There seems to be some sort of kid code whereby if one child has an injury, the other children within earshot must match it or share an even worse ailment. So instead of looking at one scraped knee, I end up looking at three scrapes in various stages of healing. It's exhausting.

Having fielded so many minor medical problems over the years has definitely impacted the way I respond. Usually, my kids will hear one of two responses from me: "Do you need a Band-Aid?" or "Have you had enough water today?" Sometimes I'll ask both for good measure. Of course, if a true emergency arises or a child is actually sick, I'll give them the necessary attention, but sometimes it's hard to determine at the moment—the dramatic wailing sounds the same.

My problem-solving responses don't stop at health complaints. I'm quick with a solution to homework challenges, friend conflicts, clothing mismatches, and a lack of snack options. If you come to me with an unsolved problem, my first instinct is to fix it, make it go away, or offer a simple three-step strategy to ease the discomfort.

Can I tell you how effective this response is at the moment? Not effective at all.

In all my years of parenting, I have yet to hear a child respond, "Thanks, Mom. That is an amazing solution I never considered before. You are so intelligent. That's why I came to you with my problem—I was looking for logic and reasoning."

More often than not, a simple solution is met with, "You don't get it! You think this is easy? You never listen! You'll never understand." Sometimes this is accompanied by yelling, aggression, and door slamming. Not exactly the result I am looking for.

Think about a time when you shared something difficult with a friend. How did they respond? How did it make you feel?

Let's imagine your friend listened intensely and then replied with, "When that happened to me . . ." and carried on talking about their own experience. Or maybe they said, "You should . . ." and then gave a strategy that ignores the nuance of your situation. Or, maybe they minimized your experience: "That's nothing. I have a friend who really struggled . . ."

You would leave this conversation feeling unheard, unknown, frustrated, confused, or more alone than you did initially.

Now imagine your friend listened intensely and then replied with empathy: "That sounds so overwhelming." To keep the conversation going, your friend encouraged you to continue talking and sharing your experience using their body language, a knowing look on their face, and phrases like "Tell me more."

You would leave this conversation feeling heard and known. You may not have solutions, your situation may still be the same, but you know you're not alone.

This is the gift we want to give our children. The gift of empathy.

## WHAT IS EMPATHY?

Empathy is about relationships. It's not a parenting "strategy." True empathy comes when we are willing to enter another person's experience with curiosity, not judgment. It's being willing to explore why this is important to them and why it causes them so much emotional distress and being willing to sit in this discomfort with them without offering a simple solution or fixing the problem. When we respond with empathy, we send our children the message "Your struggle is important. I am present with you in this challenging situation."

For many parents, this is not the default response. We're used to problem-solving, fixing things, and seeing the situation from a logical point of view. Sitting in big emotions and unsolved problems can be uncomfortable. Many of us see reason as the most helpful solution. The thinking goes, "If our children could see the situation rationally, they would realize their emotional response was out of proportion, and they would settle down." Unfortunately, emotions are rarely logical. If we're looking for ways to decrease the emotional intensity of a situation, it is better to meet emotion with empathy than to respond to emotion with logic. When you offer your child an empathetic response, you make space for big feelings—even "illogical" ones. Your child has the opportunity to feel known and understood. And you have the opportunity to support them through their challenging situation.

In most situations, your child does not want your advice. No matter how wise it is. What they want is a relationship. Their emotional response is not saying, "Fix this!"; it's saying, "See this."

This is often easier said than done. It's difficult to see the significance of a particular pair of pants or understand the complicated social network of middle school friendships. It takes effort to put your own agenda aside and agree to look at the situation through our child's eyes.

Thankfully, we do not have to agree with our child's perspective to offer empathy. In fact, there will be many times when the empathetic response you offer contradicts your viewpoint completely. For example, it's time to leave the park, you have to start dinner, and honestly, you're tired of watching them do tricks on the monkey bars. Your child doesn't share your concerns; they want to keep playing. Offering an empathetic response in this situation may sound like "You're not ready to leave. You wish you could have more time at the park." It doesn't change the fact that it's time to head home. But it does let your child know that you can see the situation from their perspective. You're not using logic to justify a decision or forcing your child to see things rationally. You're joining them in their feelings, even though you disagree.

Being empathetic to your child's perspective doesn't mean you're condoning it. Saying, "You really felt like hitting your sister" is not the same as saying, "It's OK to hit your sister." Of course you don't want your kids to hit in anger, but you can recognize that the impulse to hit is a normal reaction, especially for someone who struggles with regulation. Offering empathy gives us permission to feel a full range of emotions. Even ones that make us feel uncomfortable. It reminds them that it is OK to feel something, even if it doesn't necessarily make sense: "I'm tired and I don't want to go to bed."

Empathy is not a cure-all. It doesn't make pain, sadness, anger, or other big feelings go away. It's not a sneaky way to end a tantrum or a trick to get a child to comply. In fact, you may be the most empathetic parent and your child will still struggle with self-regulation. However, there is comfort in knowing you are not alone. There is validation when someone names our experience. Being known and seen can decrease the intensity of emotions. It can help to turn off your child's alarm, bringing them back to calm. Once your child feels heard, they may be more willing to problem-solve together and be more open to learning how to manage difficult situations, big emotions, and challenging conversations.

This is one step toward healthy communication in your home. It's about building, strengthening, or rebuilding a safe, positive relationship with your child by hearing their concerns without offering solutions. Even when you don't necessarily agree with their point of view.

## HOW TO EXPRESS EMPATHY

Empathy is the second step in healthy communication because it requires us to start with listening. To be truly empathetic, we need to become good listeners. We not only need to listen to things that are said but also need to become proficient at reading between the lines, hearing what our children cannot—or do not—put into words.

If that feels overwhelming, take a deep breath. You do not need to be amazing at empathy immediately. It may take some trial and error before you get the hang of it. And that is OK.

Start by talking less. If you find yourself launching into a lengthy lecture, resorting to logic, or laying out all the rational reasons a particular solution makes sense, this is a sign you are talking too much. Yes, you have knowledge you want to convey to your children. There will be time for that. But for now, your focus is on listening with curiosity. Your goal is not to solve the problem, but to see it from your child's perspective. Think to yourself: Why is this difficult for my child? What emotion are they feeling right now? What is it about this situation that makes them feel this way? How would I feel if I was in the same situation? How would I like someone to respond? Use this curiosity to inform your next move.

Here are a few empathetic responses:

- Use body language. Your nonverbal cues are important. Put your phone away so you can give your child your full attention. Sit down so you're at their eye level. Mirror their emotion with your face or body.

- Name their experience. Sometimes putting a child's frustration into your own words helps them know you understand. Paraphrase what you hear them saying using their words, your own, or a combination of both: "This homework assignment seems pointless."

- Put a feeling to it. Help your child build their emotional intelligence by connecting physical reactions and words to the underlying emotions. Sometimes you have to guess the emotion; it's OK if you get it wrong. "That sounds lonely," or "I bet that was embarrassing."

- Use fewer words. It's easy to turn an empathetic phrase into a lecture. There's a tendency to add,

"but you ...," or "if you only ...," or "why didn't
you think about ..." Keep your responses short.
Remember, it's not about your solutions; it's
about your child's experience.

· Keep them talking. Phrases like "Tell me more"
can encourage a child to work through their
situation or find clarity. Nonverbal responses
such as nodding, saying "mm-hmm," or showing
interest or emotion on your face also may keep
the conversation going.

· Make space for silence. Sitting next to your child,
rubbing their back, pulling them in for a hug, or
snuggling together on the couch may encourage
the conversation to continue. Even if you're
sitting in silence, it can reassure them that no
matter what they share, you are willing
to listen.

· Avoid solving the problem. This is not the time
for logic, reasoning, or teaching. Stay focused on
listening and connecting, and leave the problem-
solving for later.

Remember, this is about a relationship. Saying a sarcastic
"Wow, you look really mad" or repeating "You seem upset"
ten times in a row is probably not going to make your child
feel seen or understood. As you build empathy into your
conversations, you may find that you naturally gravitate toward
one response over another. You may find that your children

respond to a particular response and react to another. Some situations call for silence while others call for empathy. Let this be a learning experience for you and your kids. If you are conveying curiosity, listening, and working to see the situation from your child's perspective, you're doing empathy "right."

## EMPATHY WITH OURSELVES

Sitting in another person's pain is difficult. It requires emotional maturity and emotional health from the listener. It requires that we set aside our agenda, our timeline, and our need for control, to sit in this messy and complicated thing called life. We may feel that we don't have time to be empathetic or that showing empathy is coddling. Perhaps you did not experience empathy when you truly needed it.

These are all valid responses.

If empathy stretches you as a parent, this is the perfect opportunity to practice empathy . . . with yourself.

Yes.

Sometimes, the most difficult step is showing ourselves empathy. Allowing ourselves to struggle, to learn, to grow, to get it wrong. Giving ourselves grace when we talk too much. Solving the problem instead of sitting in the discomfort. Offering advice when a hug would have been enough.

Listen to your internal dialogue in these situations. How do you treat yourself? Are you critical? Do you punish yourself? Do you expect yourself to do better or be better or be someone you're not? Do you make excuses or minimize your experiences?

What if, instead, you practiced empathy with yourself? What if you gave yourself the same responses you would give your child or a close friend? How would that sound?

"It's normal to feel overwhelmed at the end of a busy day."

"That sounds very stressful."

"It's not easy to manage so many things at once."

"How exhausting!"

"It's OK to cry."

"You regret your reaction."

"It was important to you, but it didn't work out. That's disappointing."

"Ugh. That feels unfair!"

"You are not alone."

Maybe you even give yourself a hug.

If empathy is a struggle for you, it may be helpful to seek support from a mental health provider. There are many reasons people are uncomfortable sitting with another person's big feelings. It doesn't mean there is something wrong with you. Working through this yourself first will allow you to more freely offer empathy to others, including your children.

OK. We've listened, we've been empathetic. Now it's time for us to share our wisdom and solutions, right? Nope. Now we learn how to keep our kids talking.

## IT STARTS WITH YOU

- What are your go-to phrases when your kids show a big feeling?

- Which empathetic responses seem the most natural for you?

- Is there a situation where you can offer yourself empathy today?

CHAPTER 18

# Opening Up the Conversation

**Trying to have a productive conversation** with our kids can seem like an impossible task.

Can you relate to this exchange?

PARENT: How was school?
CHILD: Fine.
PARENT: What do you mean, "fine"?
CHILD: It was fine, good. Whatever.
PARENT: Was it fine or good?
CHILD: I don't know!
PARENT: How was your math test? Was Sadie on the bus? Did you turn in your permission slip? Do you have any homework? Empty your lunchbox. The dog needs to be walked.
CHILD: Leave me alone.
PARENT: Don't talk to me like that, young lady!

Or maybe this one . . .

PARENT: Anna said you broke her new headphones.
CHILD: I didn't do it!

171

PARENT: Well, she said you did.

CHILD: She's a liar!

PARENT: We do not call people names in this family!

CHILD: You always take her side!

PARENT: No, I do not. I saw you wearing the headphones yesterday.

CHILD: I didn't break them!

PARENT: Well, then who did?

CHILD: How should I know? Maybe she did. Stop blaming me!

PARENT: That's enough. You're grounded until you can buy her a new pair.

CHILD: That is so unfair! I hate you!

Not exactly our finest relationship moments.

The last two chapters have focused on being quiet, listening, and seeing things from your child's perspective. This is a lot of silence. As parents, we are used to filling the empty spaces with words of wisdom and practical solutions. Holding our tongues can be uncomfortable. You may feel like you should say something or you need to teach a lesson, give a consequence, or get to the root of the problem.

Let me give you permission not to fill this space. If you want to build connection with your kids, you need to make room for their words. We cannot get to know another person if we're always finishing their sentences. We cannot empower them to solve problems if we are always providing the solution. And we cannot build a relationship when only one person is talking.

Finding the right amount of "space" in a conversation may be something you can only determine through trial and error. A pause allows time for thinking and processing. Some people can formulate a cohesive thought in a short time, while others, including children with immature brains, often struggle with this task. When we slow down and focus on opening the conversation, it gives the other person's brain the opportunity to think, process, formulate words, and communicate them.

Even if your child is nonverbal or struggles to express thoughts and feelings, giving space models good communication skills. It demonstrates that a healthy conversation involves pausing, waiting, and listening to the other person. When you practice often, children can learn to feel comfortable in the silence rather than feeling the need to fill it with words.

Knowing when to speak is not about waiting a correct amount of time but about sending the message "I am here to listen. I want to hear your perspective. I am in no rush."

This is easier said than done. Some kids are quiet, some communicate nonstop. Some don't know how to express themselves; some are extremely expressive about everything. Opening up conversations is not about forcing our kids to become someone they are not. It's also not about you being something you're not. Knowing your child, knowing yourself, and recognizing the unique things you each bring to a conversation will help as you decide your new role as an active listener and healthy communicator.

## WATCH YOUR REACTIONS

Launching into a conversation requires more than a script or words to use. We need to be aware of what we are bringing to the table. Two things can determine if a conversation is productive or if it goes off the rails: our assumptions and our reactions.

Let's start with assumptions. Even though you may not ascribe to the old adage "children should be seen and not heard," this belief may still cloud your communication. You may outwardly encourage your kids to come to you when something is bothering them or when they have a problem, but what happens when they disagree? What happens if they share a different opinion? What if they don't listen to your advice? What if they talk back?

For many parents, these responses trigger our alarm system. Suddenly, our brain feels threatened and we're on the defense. We don't mind our kids standing up for themselves with bullies at school, but we don't want them to practice this with us at home.

Maybe, even without consciously knowing it, you feel that, as the adult, your advice, teaching, or logic should be the end of the discussion. No further dialogue necessary. Parents should have the last word. Period.

You may be carrying a number of different opinions about how children should act, react, or respond in a conversation. We talked about noticing and naming these assumptions in chapter 16. The more often you can identify them and how they impact your response, the easier it will be for you to decide to react differently. For example, if your child talks back, your first reaction may be, "I can't let her talk to me like that!" Take a deep breath. Remind yourself that big emotions are expressed when the brain is in an alarm state, these words are not coming from the thinking part of the brain. Ignoring her words in the heat of the moment gives everyone a chance to calm down and think clearly. Rewrite your assumptions so they align with the calm, confident parenting you're working toward: "I want to give my child space to express her emotions, even big and uncomfortable ones. I will talk to her about other ways to express anger without hurting others another time, when she's calm."

If your child expresses a different opinion, you may overreact because their point of view makes you question yourself or makes you feel as though you have to dig in your heels. You may have never been given space to share a unique perspective or opinion when you were a kid, so the thought of letting your child do so triggers your assumption that "parents should have the final say no matter what." Rewriting this statement may take some time, but eventually, you may be able to say, "I will show my child respect by listening and asking questions to learn more. We each see things from a different point of view. And that is normal and OK."

In addition to your assumptions, your reaction matters. If you care about creating a safe place for your child to communicate big feelings—even the uncomfortable ones— you need to be aware of the message your reaction sends.

If you lose your cool, yell at your child, correct them, or minimize their experience, they may not feel comfortable showing their true feelings in the future. If you jump to simple solutions, expect immediate compliance, or dole out consequences without understanding the problem, your child may be afraid to make a mistake. They may not learn problem-solving skills, the ability to negotiate, or how to navigate complicated social situations. If you cry, beg, or overreact, your child may feel the need to step into the caregiver role rather than let you care for them.

You do not need to be a robot parent. You are entitled to your own feelings. Even big feelings. You do not need to be a calm presence 100 percent of the time. The goal is not perfection. The goal isn't even to eliminate all conflict from your home. It's about making small changes in a positive direction. It's about being willing to step away from the conversation so you can calm down. Or, counting to twenty in your head before you respond. It's about learning to manage your big feelings in difficult conversations some of the time, and then, eventually, most of the time. It's about practicing respectful communication so people can safely share different opinions without shame. If you need to cry, scream, vent, or complain to another adult or a mental health professional, please do!

## GET YOUR KIDS TALKING

OK. We know we're going to listen, make space, and offer empathy. We're not going to use logic or reasoning or jump to a solution. I know you're eager to know what to say instead, but at this point, we still want our kids to be the ones doing the talking.

The goal is to get as much information about your child's perspective without making judgments, assumptions, or overreactions. Yes, you probably have an idea of what is going on. (Or you may be able to make a good guess.) Yes, you may be able to see a clear solution. But you want your child to understand what's going on inside, you want to empower them to communicate it well, and you want them to begin learning how to formulate a path forward.

One way to expand and open conversations is by using open-ended questions. These questions usually require a longer response rather than a one-word answer, or yes or no. Instead of "How was your science test?" you may say, "What was the most difficult part of your science test?" Instead of asking, "Did you have a good day?" you may try, "What made you smile today?" Whatever information they share can be a jumping-off point for your next open-ended question.

Empathy is also a great way to keep our children talking. Most people want to be heard and understood. They want to know that their perspective is valued. It feels good to have someone listen, especially if we feel wronged. Instead of "Why did you hit your brother?" you may put his experience into words: "You looked very frustrated when your brother took your toy." Or, instead of assuming that is the end of the story, you may say, "Tell me more." You can acknowledge their pain without solving the problem: "That sounds really difficult." Sitting nearby, holding their hand, or rubbing their back may send the message "I'm still here to listen if there's more you'd like to share."

As your kids grow, their challenges often grow with them. Suddenly, things aren't as simple as a squabble with a sibling or being unable to find a missing toy. If your older child comes to you asking for help, showing a big feeling, or presenting a challenging situation, start by asking, "Do you want solutions, or do you just want me to listen?" Asking this question clarifies your role, helping you stay present in the conversation, only moving to problem-solving if your child requests it. As the conversation progresses, you can also ask, "Is there anything else you want me to know?" This lets your child know that you want to have all the facts, to make sure you understand things from their perspective before you give advice.

Keep in mind, every child is different. Some children will give one-word answers even to open-ended questions. Some children won't share a story about their day, even if you ask nicely. Knowing your child is key to opening up the conversation. If your child is more reserved, they may have difficulty expressing their thoughts out loud. They may prefer writing their responses in a shared journal or texting back and forth. They may feel more comfortable talking in the car or in a dark bedroom so they can avoid eye contact. They may need more time and space to truly think about their response. If your child is on the quieter side, don't panic. Be curious about the best way to engage in conversation, and celebrate the times they feel comfortable sharing with you.

## CONVERSATION DO-OVERS

Here's another way these conversations could go . . .

PARENT: How was school?
CHILD: Fine.
PARENT (SMILING, KNOWING THEY NEED QUIET TIME AFTER SCHOOL): Let's find you a snack.
CHILD (EATING A SNACK, FIVE MINUTES LATER): I got a ninety-two on my math test!
PARENT: That's great! What was the hardest problem?
CHILD: I got stuck on a word problem about trains . . .

And this one . . .

PARENT: Anna's headphones are broken.
CHILD: I didn't do it!
PARENT: I'm not sure what happened to them. I know it's easy to pull too hard on the cord.
CHILD: Yeah, that happened to mine, remember?

PARENT: Yes. How did you feel when yours broke?
CHILD: I was so mad! I couldn't use them anymore!
PARENT: I wonder how Anna feels.
CHILD: I don't know. Mad, probably.
PARENT: Yeah, probably. Any idea how to help her feel better?
CHILD: No.
PARENT (REALIZING THE CHILD IS TUNING OUT): OK. Let me
   know if you think of any ideas.

Pushing the child to confess isn't going to move the conversation forward in a positive direction. The child may feel bad about breaking the headphones, but since the parent didn't shame them for that behavior, they paved the way for the child to apologize and make it right with their sister. If they are tuning out because their attention span is limited, the parent can come back to the conversation later, picking up from where they left off. If breaking his sister's things is a constant problem, the parent can do some problem-solving with him at a later time. Expanding the conversation doesn't mean having an hour-long lecture. It means making space for the child's voice to be heard.

Opening up a conversation with your child may take time. You may realize that you've been talking too much and need to step back. You may need to get comfortable sitting in silence. You may notice that your child needs more prompts or more open-ended questions to keep talking. You may have to listen to your child talk about the book they just read or the entire backstory to their LEGO creation before they will ever talk to you about a feeling. Be patient with the process. And with yourself in the process.

It's OK if it's awkward and clumsy at first. Grace-based parenting means you have lots of room to grow, learn, make mistakes, and try something new.

And since we're learning new things, let's talk about problem-solving with our kids.

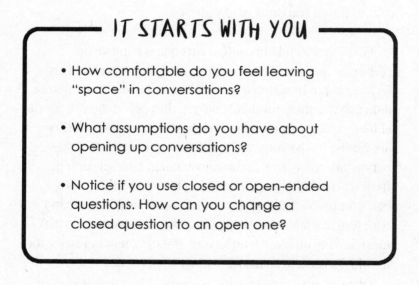

**IT STARTS WITH YOU**

- How comfortable do you feel leaving "space" in conversations?

- What assumptions do you have about opening up conversations?

- Notice if you use closed or open-ended questions. How can you change a closed question to an open one?

CHAPTER 19

# Problem-Solving Together

**The fight echoed through the house.** I ran to the
basement, afraid someone was going to get hurt. Immediately,
both girls started blaming each other. "She started it!" One girl
lunged at the other and I could feel my patience wearing thin
as I stepped between the two. Their fights had become more
frequent lately, and I was tired of playing the referee.

"Take a break. Both of you." I stated, firmly.

Both girls protested. Suddenly, their frustration was
directed toward me. "You don't even care! She's not playing
by the rules!"

"I do care, but I cannot listen to this fighting for one more
minute. We're done. Take a break. We'll talk about it later."

I walked out of the room, the only way to keep myself from
yelling. No one was happy with my solution. One child ran off
crying, the other followed me, repeating her grievances and
blaming her sister.

In the moment, all I could think about was putting a stop to
the screaming. I just wanted the big emotions to go away so we
could all get back to a peaceful home. My own anger was rising
and, selfishly, I didn't want to put in the extra energy required
to sit with them as they processed this event. My solution didn't

actually solve the problem. Sure, maybe it stopped the outburst, but this problem will pop up again soon. Did anyone learn how to handle it differently next time? No.

It's our job as parents to guide our children as they learn to navigate difficult situations. We often take this job seriously—setting consistent limits and boundaries, offering logical solutions, and jumping in before things get too difficult, uncomfortable, or frustrating. There's nothing wrong with offering your child a solution from time to time. However, problem-solving together has benefits that will stick with your child for a lifetime.

The idea of problem-solving with your child may feel very different from what you're doing now. But don't panic. It's OK for this to be a learning process. When we collaborate with our kids, we take a look at the problem from all perspectives—ours and our children's. We listen to their side of the story and share ours. Then we work together to find a solution that meets both of our needs. It's not negotiating. It's not giving in. It's not "my way or nothing." It's a conversation.

When you problem-solve with your child, you send the message "Your needs and wants are important to me. Your perspective matters." Let's face it, the typical solutions to challenging situations often work to the parent's benefit. Saying "no snacks until dinner" only takes the parent's perspective into account. We don't want our kids spoiling their appetites for the dinner we are preparing. Yes, it may be the most "logical" response, in your opinion, but it doesn't take the child's perspective into account. A solution like this shuts down communication. In fact, it may even make your child angrier! The goal of collaborative problem-solving is to find a mutually beneficial solution, which means it works for everyone—not just the parent.

Problem-solving together gives your children the opportunity to hone their communication skills. Kids need practice reading body language, monitoring tone of voice, listening to understand, and creating solutions that work for everyone involved. Every time we jump in with a solution, we rob our kids of an opportunity to improve these skills. You may be worried that problem-solving will take too much time and energy. Yes, initially, it may take a little more energy on your part. But consider how much time you spend fighting with your kids, repeating yourself thousands of times, only for your children to ignore your request. And coming up with solutions that don't actually work in the long run. Wouldn't you rather spend this time helping your child become a more respectful, nuanced, empathetic communicator?

Communication is not the only area of growth your child can find through collaborative problem-solving. Allowing your children to feel a full range of emotions—without jumping in to "save" them with a solution—can also improve their self-regulation. Remember, you cannot rush self-regulation, but you can give your child opportunities to practice with your support. I know it's difficult to see your child struggling. Solving the problem may seem like a compassionate thing to do. Unfortunately, when your child escapes the big feelings, they also skip the opportunity to practice coping and calming skills. They miss the opportunity to think through their choices, examine the consequences, and make a calm and educated decision. Your willingness to brainstorm solutions together can be a compassionate response, letting them know you will be there to support them through big emotions, as well as anything that happens as a result of their decision.

Problem-solving together makes room for the child to feel heard, seen, loved, and understood. Taking the time to listen and offer empathy means we are willing to step into our child's experience and see things from their point of view. Stopping the conversation long enough to make space gives your child an opportunity to use their voice. Maybe they will share something important you never considered. Maybe you will gain insight into their challenges and growth areas. Or maybe you will recognize that your child wasn't looking for a solution; they simply needed a listening ear.

## PROBLEM-SOLVING STEP-BY-STEP

Problem-solving with your child may be a new and uncomfortable communication challenge. You may wonder how your child will respond, fear being too permissive, or worry about being judged by others who do not parent with the same intention. These are all normal reactions. Be kind to yourself as you learn how to work together with your child rather than against them. Remind yourself that grace-based parenting means being willing to communicate with calm confidence, seeing our kids as worthy of a respectful conversation, even if we don't necessarily see eye-to-eye.

If you're reading this book chronologically, you've already set the stage for productive problem-solving with your kids. Everything we've worked on to this point will help you be present in this conversation. A calm brain, connected relationships, and good listening skills are key to problem-solving well. If you are still working on any of these areas, don't feel pressured to move on to this step. Take your time. Get the support you need to stay present in difficult conversations, especially if your child struggles to respond respectfully or is not willing to engage in a dialogue with you.

## EMPATHY

Every good conversation starts with a willingness to listen to the other person's perspective. Often, we appear to be listening, but we are actually formulating a response or a witty comeback! Remember, empathy means seeing something from your child's perspective, or putting yourself in their shoes, even if you do not agree with their opinions or feelings.

Sometimes we start with empathy but immediately switch to problem-solving: "You don't want to take a bath (empathy) . . . Well, you're dirty from playing in the yard today (logic) . . . so you have to take a bath tonight (solution)." Yes, your child may be dirty and yes, a bath may be on your agenda for him tonight, but at this point in the problem-solving process, we want to stay focused on his perspective. "You don't want to take a bath tonight, huh?" Pause. "It's hard to stop playing, isn't it?" Let him know you understand that this is a big deal.

Empathy also can get offtrack when we minimize our child's experience. Sayings like "Calm down" or "It's not that bad" can put an abrupt end to a conversation. In other words, "A solution isn't needed here; you're fine." It's normal to be overwhelmed with a child's emotion or to be too busy, tired, or irritated to want to address it. However, if we want to move toward a collaborative solution, we need to set our own inconveniences aside and embrace our child's big feelings.

In the empathy step, your job is to make sure you understand the problem from your child's perspective. Using good listening skills, you can keep your child talking until you think you have a good handle on the whole situation. Questions like "Is there anything else you'd like me to know?" or "Am I getting it?" ensure your child feels heard and that you've heard all they're willing to share without rushing to conclusions or making assumptions.

## DEFINING THE PROBLEM

Step two gives you and your child an opportunity to lay out your concerns as they apply to this challenging situation. This may be the most difficult step because it requires you to be aware of your tendency to problem-solve and to be willing to hear your child's grievances.

We've talked a lot about assumptions we bring to conversations, and this is another area where they impact communication. We assume we know or understand our children's perspectives without needing more information. Without knowing or hearing their points of view, we create solutions that don't work. "You're having trouble getting up for school. I'm going to buy you a louder alarm clock" may sound like a logical solution, but it relies on an assumption (she must not be hearing her alarm clock) that may or may not be true. And it may or may not have anything to do with why she's struggling to wake up for school. When you practice "defining the problem," you want to keep the conversation open-ended. Authors Ross Greene and J. Stuart Ablon suggest starting with a phrase like "I've noticed" and ending with the question, "what's up?"[1] So in this situation, you may say, "I've noticed you're having trouble getting up for school. What's up?" Then leave space to listen, and use empathy and open-ended questions to learn more.

In a similar way, parents often forget to clearly communicate our own concerns—skipping right to solutions instead. "No TV after dinner" is a solution without a clear concern. If we step back and work to uncover the actual concern, it may be, "When you watch TV after dinner, it's difficult for you to transition to the bedtime routine. We argue so long that you get to bed late, and that means you're not getting enough sleep." The parent's concern is actually about quality sleep. Removing TV seems like the most logical solution, but taking it away may or may not affect the child's ability to sleep well. Problem-solving together means both concerns—yours and theirs—need to be clarified before solutions are discussed. When we model sharing our concerns with our kids, we can help them learn to identify and communicate their own as well.

## BRAINSTORMING TOGETHER

Now that your child feels heard and both your and your child's concerns are clearly defined, you can move on to the problem-solving step. Problem-solving can only come after calming our brains, connecting, and listening. It's easy to jump to problem-solving right away; many of us do it without even being aware of our intentions. If you notice you're giving solutions before listening, take a deep breath and start over.

Step three, according to Greene and Ablon, "involves *inviting* the child to collaboratively brainstorm ideas for solving the problem in a way that is *feasible* and *mutually satisfactory*. The invitation makes it clear that solving the problem is something child and adult are doing together."[2] This means the solution needs to work for everyone, and each person must be able to follow through with their part. It's not necessarily about negotiating or finding a "middle ground"; it's about having a conversation that leads to a workable solution. You can model that this is a conversation by inviting your child into the brainstorming—"Do you have any suggestions for solving this problem?"—rather than jumping in with your own solution or advice.

Work together to create a list of potential solutions. Write down any of your child's suggestions. Then add a few of your own. This is your chance to be creative, out-of-the-box thinkers. It's OK if your kids struggle to find solutions initially. This is a skill that takes practice before it becomes second nature. If their suggestions don't work for you, you may need to say, "That addresses your concern, but it doesn't address mine." And vice versa. A solution needs to be "feasible," which means each person actually needs to be able to do it. If a solution isn't feasible, you need to point that out: "I'm not sure ten minutes is enough time to get ready for school. Let's keep thinking."

Once you have narrowed down your list, pick a solution to try. Be aware that the first solution is rarely the best solution. It usually takes time—and more conversations—to find a solution that actually works for everyone and can be carried out without a struggle. Be patient. If you try something for a few days and it doesn't work, head back to the drawing board. Start back at the empathy step: "I've noticed you're still having trouble turning off the Xbox; what's up?" See what you missed, brainstorm more ideas, or try another solution from the original list.

## PROBLEM-SOLVING TOGETHER

Collaborative problem-solving isn't only for children and parents. It can also be used to help siblings find a solution to their challenges. Going back to the fight in the basement, I could have entered the room with a calm brain, recognizing that their big emotions didn't require a huge emotional response from me.

"Whoa. It's getting loud down here; what's up?"

Both kids start pointing the finger at each other. Blaming each other.

Taking another deep breath, I hold out my arms. "OK. I want to hear each side, but I can't listen well when everyone is yelling. Are you ready to talk this through now, or should we calm down first?"

"Now." They both agree. Still fuming.

I start with empathy. "It seems like you're upset about the game. Can you help me understand what happened?"

Both girls share their experiences. I do my best to help them focus on their own experience and listen to each other without interrupting. "OK, let me see if I get it. You feel like she ended the game too quickly, and you were tired of playing the game? Is that it?" They nod.

"Do you have any ideas for solving this problem?" I ask.

They struggle to find a solution, coming up with only one idea: "She could give me some warning before she wants to stop."

Thankfully, they both agree.

I'm not sure it will be a long-term solution, but it's something to try in the meantime. The bigger win is giving them the opportunity to practice problem-solving together, seeing disagreements and challenges not as something to be avoided but as the beginning of a grace-filled conversation.

Sometimes, our conversations will flow beautifully; other times, they may feel clumsy, and we may fall back into old habits of yelling or jumping to conclusions. The next chapter will walk through common communication challenges.

## IT STARTS WITH YOU

- What concerns do you have about problem-solving together?

- In what ways do you see problem-solving together being a benefit to your family?

- Which step seems the most difficult: empathy, defining the problem, or brainstorming?

# CHAPTER 20

# Troubleshooting Communication

**The last few chapters have stripped** away common parenting strategies, such as lecturing, repeating, and using logic to defend our decisions. You may be feeling uneasy with all the listening and silence and hearing your child's point of view. It's a different way of approaching challenging behavior, and it may take some time before it feels natural to you. If you've relied on yelling or repeating or giving in as your go-to parenting strategy for a while, you may find yourself falling back into those habits, even as you attempt to put new habits into place. Again, that's totally normal. Learning how to have a respectful conversation takes time and practice. Give yourself lots of grace as you take it one step at a time.

Here are a few common communication problems and suggestions for how to respond.

## I'M BEING RESPECTFUL, BUT MY KIDS ARE NOT

One of the most difficult parts of changing communication in our home is waiting for our kids to catch on. We cannot force our kids to communicate respectfully, but we can model the behavior we'd like to see. Changing the way your family communicates starts with you. Rather than pointing out the ways your kids are being disrespectful, focus on your own communication first. Make sure you're not falling into old habits like yelling, using sarcasm, eye-rolling, or mocking.

When your child is disrespectful, you have an opportunity to use all the skills we've been learning here. Disrespectful language often triggers our alarm response. Be aware of how your body responds—are you tense? Is your brain preparing for a fight? Do you have a sudden urge to run away and avoid the conversation? As you notice these reactions, remind yourself that this is a normal brain reaction to a threatening situation. Go back to your calming ideas and choose a few that will allow you to stay present with your child, if possible. Do what you can to model respectful behavior, even when your child is struggling.

Your first instinct may be that a disrespectful child needs immediate correction and consequences. Giving a punishment for disrespectful language often perpetuates challenging behavior, leading to even more disrespect. Instead, I'd encourage you to start with empathy and listening. A child who is choosing words that hurt others is often experiencing a big emotion inside. Sometimes this behavior triggers the shame spiral, reiterating that they are a "bad kid." Big feelings may mean that your child is in the alarm state, being on alert and scanning the environment for threats. Recognizing that your child is in fight or flight mode may be a reminder that they need your calm presence to regulate their emotions. Offering a listening ear, hearing their underlying hurt or pain, or seeing things from their perspective—even if you do not agree—are all ways to demonstrate respectful communication and help your child's brain return to calm.

It's not easy to stay present with a child who is being disrespectful. Especially if they are saying things intentionally meant to hurt your feelings. In these situations, you may need to work even harder on your self-talk, reminding yourself that you are not defined by your child's hurtful words or rewriting the phrases so they are accurate. ("I am not the meanest mom ever. I am a mom who cares. I am a mom who is involved. I am a mom who prioritizes listening over being right.") Once the dust has settled and your child is back to calm, you can have a problem-solving conversation together about different ways to express big emotions. Your child may need suggestions for ways to manage their frustrations, talk about their feelings, or disagree respectfully.

Even though you may not notice an overnight change in your child's conversation, calm, empathetic responses make a difference with time. Rather than preparing for a fight, your child may be less reactive, recognizing that you are there to help, not to engage in an argument. Feeling seen, heard, and understood can break through the shame spiral, allowing your child to drop their defenses and admit when they were wrong or if they need help. Problem-solving together shows your child that their ideas are important and that you value their perspective. Rather than looking for an immediate change in communication, notice times when your child responds with respect. Thank them for being willing to talk about a problem without getting angry. Or, be aware of conversations that start off tense but end on a positive note.

If you've tried modeling respectful communication and your child continues to struggle with disrespect, it may be time to seek support from a mental health provider. It doesn't mean you have failed or you have somehow caused this behavior. Sometimes it takes an outside perspective to change communication patterns in a family. Getting help is a sign that you know your limits and acknowledge the need for additional support.

## MY CHILD DOESN'T RESPOND WELL TO EMPATHY

Sometimes, hearing our emotions named by another person is healing. It's freeing. When a caregiver points out that a child looks sad, the tears start to fall and they are able to cry freely, feeling relieved when the cry is over. But for other children, this outpouring of emotion can be overwhelming. They don't want to experience a big feeling, especially one that comes on suddenly. Some children are resistant to hearing emotions named because it triggers a shame response. Their internal dialogue tells them that they are a "bad kid" because they're feeling angry, sad, frustrated, or discouraged. Rather than embracing this feeling as a normal part of the human experience, these children refuse to let their caregivers name this emotion. When a child's brain is in the alarm state, even kind gestures can be misinterpreted as threats. They may push away your attempts to connect or reject your kind words. Even though you can clearly see the scowl on their face, clenched fists, and hear their screaming, your child remains adamant that they are "not angry."

It can be confusing.

Don't panic. Take a deep breath. Remember, your response matters, even if your child doesn't embrace your help right away. Empathy is one way to respond when your child is upset, but it doesn't have to look or sound a particular way. If your child is resistant to your attempts at connection, that's OK. Set your empathetic responses to the side and focus on being a calm presence. See if you can connect with your child in a different way, maybe offering to share a snack, color together, or take a walk. Say something like "I love you. I'm here when you're ready." The goal is to let them know that you see things from their perspective, and in this instance, their perspective is "resist empathy." This doesn't mean you're doing something wrong, but it may mean you need to adjust your approach for the moment until their brain and body are open to accepting your kind gestures.

It's easy to overdo empathy or to respond in a way that seems "empathetic" but is actually not. Think about how you would feel if someone kept repeating, "You look angry." Chances are, at some point, you'd yell back, "Yes! I am angry! And now I'm even angrier; thanks to you for pointing it out!" When you use empathy with your children, be conscious of your responses. Use a mixture of naming the feeling, using body language, paraphrasing their responses, and saying short phrases like "Tell me more." Think about how you would like someone to respond if you were in this situation. Would you like to hear advice, or would silence be a better response? Would you like your emotion named, or would an understanding facial expression be enough?

Remember, empathy is not a strategy for ending a tantrum. It's not a sneaky way to get your child to do what you want them to do. It's about the relationship. If your child continues crying or seems more upset when you name their feelings, it may simply be that they have emotions built up inside that they need to express. It may be that you've named their feelings so acutely that it gave them permission to feel it fully. Or it may be that, even though they feel heard and understood, they still do not want to do what is being asked. All these responses are normal. It doesn't mean that empathy "didn't work," but it may be that empathy didn't have the end result you were looking for. Don't give up on empathy just because your child continues to show a big emotion. Continue to do what you can to keep the relationship strong and have respectful conversations about feelings, calming skills, and collaborative solutions.

If admitting emotions or receiving empathy is extremely difficult for your child regularly, it may be helpful to seek the support of a mental health provider. Again, this is not a failure on your part but a way you can support your child to grow mentally healthy.

## MY KIDS EXPECT ME TO SOLVE THEIR PROBLEMS
In the beginning stages of problem-solving, your kids may look at you with confusion on their faces. They may have literally zero ideas for solving the problem. Or, any ideas they do have involve forcing the other person to do things their way. Problem-solving is a learned skill like anything else. It will take time for your kids to get good at brainstorming solutions and working together to come to a mutually satisfactory idea.

If you're getting a lot of blank stares from your kids, use this as an opportunity for teaching. You can start by laying out a few silly or extraordinary solutions, "Maybe, we rip the remote in half so you can both hold it?" or "How about we eat nothing but mayonnaise for lunch today." The point is to break the tension and get your kids thinking. Then you can move the conversation forward, saying, "You're right, that's not a good idea. Do you have any suggestions?" If your child volunteers something that isn't practical, help them narrow it down in a way that keeps the spirit of their initial idea: "Getting a fridge in your room isn't going to work right now, but you've got a point. Maybe we need to clear a space in our fridge so everyone knows those are your snacks."

Sometimes kids will present us with a problem or a big feeling because they want us to fix it for them so they don't have to fix it themselves. Author Lisa Damour calls this "externalization." She says, "externalization is a technical term describing how teenagers sometimes manage their feelings by getting their parents to have their feelings instead. In other words, they toss you an emotional hot potato."[1] Instead of helping your child find solutions together, you're frantically calling teachers, attempting to smooth things over between your child and a friend, or staying up at night worrying about an upcoming school project. These are problems, but at this point, they've become your problems, not your child's. If you find yourself feeling frantic to find a solution, stop. Take a deep breath. Think back to the problem and how it got to this point. Ask yourself, Is this an "emotional hot potato?" Something your child gave you as a coping mechanism? Does this situation require this much involvement from you? Or, have you taken on more than your fair share of the problem-solving, and will you need to go back to brainstorming with your child? It's normal to throw a "hot potato," and it's normal to have the desire to jump in and help your child solve a problem. Unfortunately, in this situation, you miss the chance to help your kids manage big, uncomfortable, or overwhelming feelings.

The goal of problem-solving together is to slowly expand your child's vocabulary and ability to see different options. Decreasing the stress and tension of a situation makes space for creativity, giving them a chance to think outside the box for solutions. It may take time before you can step out of the facilitator role, and that is normal. In the meantime, look for ways to encourage and support your child's efforts and progress.

## HOW DO I SET LIMITS AND BOUNDARIES?

Many people misunderstand empathy and listening as "permissive" strategies. They think that because we are spending time hearing our children's perspectives, that means the kids can do whatever they want without consequences. In the "old" ways of parenting, limits and boundaries are often set without any concern for the child's emotional state or perspective. In grace-based parenting, limits and boundaries are not the focus; instead, it's about creating a safe, calm, and connected relationship.

A parent can still create a boundary for a child while being empathetic. Instead of saying, "No candy; it's almost bedtime," you can offer empathy: "I know you really want this candy, huh?" When the child feels heard, you can create a plan together: "It's too close to bedtime right now. Can you help me find a special place to set it until the morning?" If your child still resists, you can listen and offer comfort and support while they wrestle with the fact that they do not get to eat candy before bed.

As your child grows, implementing collaborative problem-solving is a way to navigate tricky situations that would normally lead to a family battle. This time, instead of coming at the situation with a "my way or the highway" perspective, you and your child work together. Remember, finding a mutually satisfactory solution means one that works for both people. You can still hold a limit; it just looks different than it did using your old parenting strategies because you're also taking your child's concerns into account.

Your kids need you to be the calm, confident leader of the house. But this doesn't mean you need to rule with a heavy hand. Kids who feel heard, respected, and connected to their caregivers are more likely to listen and comply with requests. We will talk about this more in the next chapter.

In the meantime, focus more on your own triggers and less on lists of rules. Focus more on modeling respectful communication than pointing out disrespectful communication. Focus more on keeping the relationship strong than holding fast to traditional parenting strategies.

And of course, give yourself permission to learn, grow, and make mistakes. Moving forward in a positive direction can be uncomfortable, but with time, you may recognize a sense of peace and increased confidence.

Imperfectly, of course. Always being kind to yourself in the process.

# IT STARTS WITH YOU

- How can you give yourself grace as you practice respectful communication?

- How do your kids respond to empathy? How do you respond to empathy?

- Can you relate to being thrown a "hot potato" problem from your kids?

# CHAPTER 21

# Be Curious

**As soon as the tension rises** in our home, my wheels start turning. I filter through a long list of potential reasons my child is struggling. Within a matter of minutes, I mentally examine her recent sleep patterns, eating habits, daily schedule, connection with caregivers, time with friends, time alone, and environmental stimulation. The answers usually give me a snapshot of why it's difficult for her to regulate at this particular moment.

But sometimes, this list leaves me with more questions than answers. She seemed to be happy earlier in the day. We spent time together. There's nothing obvious that would lead to her escalating frustration.

In these moments, I have a choice. I can make assumptions about her behavior, or I can be curious.

Traditional parenting strategies often start with assumptions: she's manipulating me, he's lazy, she knows exactly which buttons to push to get a rise out of me. Many people look to consequences as a result of these assumptions: if he's lazy, taking away his video games will make him more productive. Or, sitting her in timeout will teach her not to yell at me next time. It's frustrating when these interventions do not have the intended result. A few days later, we're still talking about the same behaviors and increasing the consequences.

What if we flipped the script? Instead of looking at the observable behaviors, let's get curious. Let's dig beyond what we can see, think beyond our assumptions, and explore the root causes of our children's behavior.

Curiosity is beneficial for two reasons: One, you can start to see patterns and maybe even begin to predict when your child is going to struggle. Two, you can create solutions that actually solve the underlying problem, not just put a Band-Aid on it and hope it goes away. Curiosity is a slow process. It requires a calm, confident caregiver. It requires patience and empathy. Connecting with your children with curiosity keeps the relationship at the forefront. It sends the message "I know you're a kid. You're growing and learning. We all make mistakes; we all struggle. I'm here to help you figure out what's going on and find a way to help you get back on track."

## CURIOUS QUESTIONS
Being curious starts with questions. If you're starting with assumptions, offering solutions, or looking for consequences, you're moving too fast. Slow down. Ask questions with nonjudgmental open-mindedness. Be truly interested in knowing the potential reasons rather than looking for an answer to prove your assumption.

Here are some questions to get you started:

- Why?

- Why now?

- What makes this time different?

- What makes this time more difficult?

- Why is this time of day/day of the week significant?

- What seems to make this behavior decrease?

- What seems to make this behavior worse?

- What need is my child expressing?

- Why is this setting significant?

- Why are these people/family members/peers significant?

- What else is going on?

- What other factors impact this response?

The answers may come quickly and easily: She struggles with self-regulation when she's hungry. This is a difficult math assignment and math does not come easily to him. Or, the answers may take more digging: Could the fact that we were out late last night influence this behavior? Could this be her way of telling me she's had a difficult day? There may be layers and layers of factors leading up to the behavior you observed, so take as many steps backward as needed to get a clear picture.

While being curious can help us adjust how we respond to our kids, we also want to teach and empower our kids to be curious about their own behavior. Noticing how their body feels, identifying challenging situations, and naming emotions help them become better problem-solvers. It also keeps them off the shame spiral, reminding them that they are not a mistake; they are human—with thoughts and actions that are impacted by the people and the environment around them. When our kids are little, we can verbalize our observations: "I notice you cover your ears when the baby cries. It's loud, huh?" Then pull her in for a cuddle to assure her she's not alone. As your kids grow, you can encourage them by saying something like "I've noticed you seem tense today; what's up?" At first, they may be defensive ("I'm not tense!") or confused ("Why do you say that?"), but with time, and your help, they may be able to recognize when the tension starts creeping into their body. Even if they can't specifically identify the cause of their tension, saying "I feel tense" is helping them move in a positive direction.

## FACTORS THAT IMPACT BEHAVIOR
As you ask questions and dig into the "why" behind your child's behavior, you may find yourself feeling stuck. Your first reaction may be "I don't know. I have no idea why he's acting this way." Or, you may take it personally: "I must be failing him as a parent." Being curious takes time and practice just like every other new skill. There are many things that impact your child's behavior; many have nothing to do with your parenting. Take a deep breath. Give yourself permission to set the judgments aside and continue to practice exploring with curiosity, not criticism.

Here are some things to consider as you search for the "why":

- lack of sleep

- hunger and thirst

- overstimulation or understimulation

- activity level

- feeling disconnected from caregivers

- big life changes (such as moving, starting a new school, death of a loved one, separation, or divorce)

- diet, allergies, and food intolerances

- learning challenges and learning style

- friendships (or lack of peer connection)

- feeling unsafe

- medical conditions, including vision and hearing challenges

- mental health diagnoses

- screen time

- fears and worries

- lack of routine, structure, or clear understanding of what comes next

- difficulty reading social cues

- insecurities and shame

- difficulty processing and expressing thoughts and feelings

- temperament and personality type

- developmental stage

This list is unique to your family, child, and living situation. And it can be different for each child in your family. One child may be impacted by something while another child barely bats an eyelash at the same concern. It's not about finding the "right" answer as much as it is about working to get a clear picture of your unique child's challenges. When we're curious, we don't go in knowing the answer. We make space to think, process, and explore.

One more thing to keep in mind: be careful of the word "just" when you're explaining the "why" behind your child's behavior. Saying "She's just tired" may be another way of saying, "Even though she's tired, I believe she should be able to manage her behavior in this situation." Instead, take out the word "just." "She's tired" is a complete sentence, and it may be at least one of the reasons your child is struggling at this moment. It's not an excuse; it's something to consider as you move toward solutions.

## CURIOSITY MOVES TO PROBLEM-SOLVING

When we are willing to be curious about behavior without jumping to conclusions or making assumptions, we are able to find solutions that meet our child's underlying needs. When we make space to stop and see the behavior from a nonjudgmental perspective, we are more empathetic and compassionate to our children's unique struggles. We are grace-first, grace-based parents.

Let's look at two examples of how curiosity can inform your response.

What you observe: Your child refuses to brush their teeth before bed. Every night, it's the same struggle. You mention teeth brushing and they ignore you. After your first five reminders are ignored, you switch to yelling, demanding they "get into the bathroom to brush their teeth!" Most nights, the fight escalates from there.

Being curious, you explore possible reasons brushing teeth is such a struggle.

- They don't know how to brush their teeth properly or forget the order of the steps.

- They have trouble with transitions (especially from a desired activity to a less desired one).

- Teeth brushing is the first sign that bedtime is coming, and they do not like being disconnected from you at night.

- Resisting teeth brushing gets your attention (even if it means you're yelling).

This list may just be the beginning. You may have even more things to add, such as their developmental stage, the sensory experience of toothbrushing, or your own triggers related to a child resisting being told what to do. Children of all ages can be encouraged to share their thoughts, feelings, and experiences. This practice encourages self-reflection and helps them identify needs and communicate them respectfully to others. You can open up the conversation, being willing to hear their perspective, even if you do not necessarily agree, saying something like "I've noticed you avoid teeth brushing in the evening. What's up?" Or, "I wonder if you have any ideas how we can make teeth brushing better?"

As you read through the list, see which one resonates most with your experience. Which one seems to best explain your child's behavior? There may be more than one explanation, and that's OK. If you miss something the first time, or your explanations don't seem to fit, you can always go back and be curious again.

Once you've considered the possibilities, you can explore the best way to respond or react. Each bullet point will need a slightly different solution. If she struggles to remember the steps required of teeth brushing, you can create a visual reminder together, and hang it in the bathroom. If she struggles with transitions, you can make sure to add extra time between activities and work on building frustration tolerance, especially around ending fun activities. If disconnection is the main concern, you can create space for one-on-one time and add more connections during the day. And if teeth brushing is your child's best way to get your attention—even negatively—it may be time to focus on calming your alarm so you can give your child positive, nonyelling attention more often.

Let's look at a second example.

What you observe: Homework is a struggle. Every night it is the same battle. Your child waits until the last minute, then pulls out a crumpled folder full of homework due the next day. Instead of working on it, they find every single distraction available. They don't stay at the table. They require your constant monitoring. Things that should only take a few minutes end up taking hours and usually end with one or both of you in tears.

Being curious, you explore why homework is such a struggle.

- Organization is a challenge.

- Math seems to come easily to them, but language does not.

- Evenings are busy; there's limited time for free play.

- Sitting still for so long at school and then again at home may not work for their body.

Again, this list would probably be much longer, especially if you opened up the conversation, listening with the intention of actually hearing their point of view. You may even talk with others who interact with them—teachers, school professionals, or other caregivers—to see if your experience is the same or different. You may dig into your own experience, exploring the feelings underneath your fears.

Your curiosity may lead to more questions than answers. How can you help them feel more organized? Would a checklist help? Or a visual timer? What exactly is difficult about the language homework—is it understanding what they are reading, putting it into their own words, processing new thoughts, handwriting, finding the letters on the keyboard? How do you best help them learn this lacking skill? How can you rearrange their schedule to incorporate more downtime? Would it help for them to stand up when they're doing homework or walk on a treadmill while reading? Would meeting with professionals—a learning specialist or occupational therapist—be a good next step?

Being curious is the starting point. It's the beginning of a conversation—or an exploration—not the end. As you become curious, you may find patterns in your child's behavior. You may notice areas where they struggle consistently across settings or environments. You may have a better sense of their needs and longings. You may have a long list of skills you'd like to teach your child—patience, frustration tolerance, communicating emotions without aggression, organization, ways to respectfully disagree, how to manage disappointment, and so on. The more curious you are, the more you will learn. And the more you learn, the better you will be at relating and responding to your child in a way that truly helps them grow.

And while we're at it, let's be curious about our own behavior too. Instead of beating ourselves up for losing our cool or giving in, take a second to wonder with some nonjudgmental curiosity: "Why did I snap at her?" Or, "What's going on today?" Or, "I wonder why I feel so much tightness in my shoulders?" Go back to chapter 8 about calm parenting and think about how stress manifests in your brain and body, and then explore your calming and coping options. Use the information you gained by being curious to meet your own needs. Do you need the support of a mental health professional? Do you need to reach out to a friend? Do you need to get to bed earlier? Or delete a social media app from your phone? Whatever it is, it is OK to have needs and to work to meet those needs. It's OK to have struggles. And it's even OK not to know what you need right now. Be kind to yourself in this process.

Practicing grace-filled responses with ourselves will help us offer grace to our children. It's not about perfection, perfect behavior, perfect responses, or even perfect curiosity. It's about grace.

The next chapter will dive deeper into assumptions that keep us from moving forward in a positive direction.

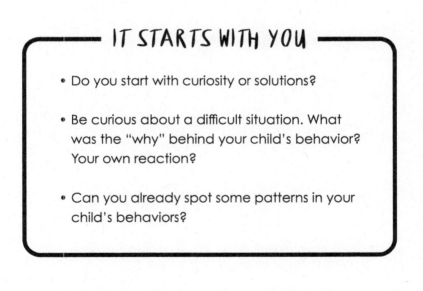

## IT STARTS WITH YOU

- Do you start with curiosity or solutions?

- Be curious about a difficult situation. What was the "why" behind your child's behavior? Your own reaction?

- Can you already spot some patterns in your child's behaviors?

# CHAPTER 22

# Change Your Perspective

**Relationship researcher John Gottman** talks about a "magic ratio" of five positive interactions to every one negative. For every negative interaction, a stable and happy relationship has five or more positive interactions. His research focuses on the marriage relationship, but it can also apply to the relationship with our children.

I call this the "nice-to-nag" ratio.

When I meet with parents for parent coaching sessions, I often ask them to think about the ratio of positive interactions versus negative interactions with their kids. "Negative" interactions may be anything from directing, redirecting, giving reminders, criticizing, using sarcasm, arguing, and yelling to physical interactions. Positive interactions are anything that speaks love to your children, things that are done and said with respect. When a family is in conflict, the ratio is usually closer to five negatives to every one positive interaction.

It's easy to slip into an unbalanced ratio. Life is busy. Often, we're rushing through our days barely noticing one another. Just existing in the same home together. If I get complacent about noticing the good things my kids are doing, I'm more likely to be hyperfocused on the negative behavior. I get nitpicky about uncompleted chores or overly upset about simple sibling squabbles.

Before I know it, it's difficult to find the good because I'm so focused on seeing those undesirable traits.

When I slow down, I notice that my ratio needs to be adjusted. One of the best ways to adjust my focus is by watching my children from a distance. I love observing them in their element. They may be playing a game of make-believe in the backyard, filming a complex movie scene on their iPhone, coloring at the kitchen table, or jamming to a favorite tune on their headphones. Just kids being kids. Living in the moment.

Adding a pause reminds us that focusing on all their imperfections is misleading. There's so much more to our kids than the fact that they leave socks everywhere or forget to turn off the bathroom light. When the ratio is balanced, you're able to see that your son is a caring friend, especially to kids who are struggling. Or notice that your animal-loving daughter takes excellent care of your pets. Sure, there are things we'd like our kids to learn or do differently, but when it comes right down to it, we are reminded that our kids are amazing just by being who they are.

Our perspective matters.

Everyone carries around an unspoken understanding of why kids act the way they do. Some of these thoughts are helpful; they drive you to pick up your crying toddler and kiss imaginary boo-boos. But some of these thoughts and beliefs keep you stuck in a parenting rut. They keep you from moving forward or trying a new parenting strategy.

## PERSPECTIVES THAT KEEP YOU STUCK

Thoughts and beliefs about how children should behave are often passed down from generation to generation. Phrases like "she's just trying to manipulate me" or "he's so spoiled" slip into our vocabulary, and it's difficult to recognize how they affect our parenting. Sometimes they're not even explicitly stated; they're just under the surface or in our subconscious. Noticing and naming these beliefs is the first step to recognizing how they impact your relationship with your child.

Read through these common phrases and see if you can relate.

### "He's Too Old For . . ."

This phrase is often used for things like sleeping with a baby blanket, missing a parent while they're away, or throwing a tantrum over something that seems minor. Variations include "Your younger sister can handle this; why can't you!" or "Do other kids in your class cry like this?" Or, it may be conveyed with your body language, as you roll your eyes because they are suddenly scared to go into the dark basement alone. At some point, we assume our children should be able to function at a more mature level and we deem their actions "childish."

The fact is, your child is childish! They are still finding their way in the world. The things that gave them comfort when they were babies or toddlers may still bring them comfort as tweens, and even teens. Since your child's brain is still developing, sometimes they will be able to handle a big feeling like sadness or frustration, and other days they may not be able to regulate enough to get through without a meltdown. This is normal.

Rather than picking an arbitrary date when your child "should" have grown out of a behavior or need, take a deep breath. Your child is growing at their own pace. Acknowledge that your child is having a "childish" day, or that they are going through a period of time where they may not act as "mature" as they usually do. Give them space to rest in the comfort of something familiar. Offer extra cuddles. Remind yourself that being a calm, confident, empathetic caregiver will help your child build resilience and give them an opportunity to practice regulation.

If you are concerned that your child isn't developing at an appropriate rate or that their behavior is outside of what would be considered typical for their age, please speak with your child's pediatrician. You may also want to reach out to a mental health provider if you feel that your child could benefit from new coping skills, strategies to overcome fears, or social skills practice.

### "She'll Never Learn!"

I can almost feel the frustration of the parent who utters this phrase. It's a feeling of desperation and exasperation mixed together. It's challenging when our kids do the same undesired behavior time and time again. Especially if you feel like you've tried everything to help them make a different choice.

It's normal to reach a point in your parenting where you don't know what to do next. It's normal to feel like you've tried everything and nothing works. It's also normal to feel overwhelmed by your child's behavior to the point where you say, "I give up."

If you find yourself in this situation—or at this level of frustration—take a deep breath. Tune into your own needs. Do you need support from a friend or a mental health professional? Do you need a break or a chance to pause? Do you need to learn a new way to teach or support her so she can be successful or move in a positive direction? You don't need to have all the answers. Getting the support you need can help you see things from a different perspective and give you the energy to support your child as they learn.

Then go back to being curious. What is getting in the way of her learning this desired task? Tune into your child, exploring how they learn, their temperament, their needs, and their challenges. Are your expectations reasonable for a child her age? Can she do what you are requesting without your support? Step back and take a brave look at your expectations and your teaching strategies. Notice if you're trying to teach in the middle of big feelings or if you wait until her brain is calm. Explore other ways to teach your child that fit better with her personality.

Work to rephrase this in a more helpful way. Maybe try, "She needs more help to master this skill." Or "She will learn. I can be patient and supportive in the process." Or "She's struggling. So am I. We'll get through this together."

### *"I Can't Let Her Get Away with That!"*
For many years, parents were told that kids need to receive a consequence—usually immediately—in order to learn that a behavior is wrong. There was a fear that waiting or delaying a consequence could send the message that the misbehavior was OK.

However, when we look at teaching from a brain perspective, we realize that in the heat of the moment, the emotional part of the brain is completely running the show.

Your child is not able to learn, problem-solve, or think logically or rationally about their behavior. Which means . . . you need to wait. By pausing, breathing, and making space to quiet the alarm, you give your child's thinking brain a chance to come back online. Children with calm brains and connected relationships are in the best position to learn from a difficult situation.

Even if you understand what's happening in your child's brain, you may still feel uneasy about waiting. It may still feel too permissive or like you are giving in. People in your community may judge you or criticize you for not doing enough in the moment. Noticing what comes up internally is a great place to start. Be aware of your own feelings and your tendency to fall back into old habits. Be kind to yourself, especially if you're feeling unsure.

Remind yourself that you're not "letting them get away" with unsafe, unkind, or undesired behavior, you're simply waiting until their brain is fully engaged in the learning process. You are still their parent and their best teacher. You're still going to be creative, curious, and calm as you help them problem-solve. You're the expert on your unique child. And by keeping the relationship with them as your priority, you know there will be time for teaching when everyone is back to calm.

### "He's Just Trying to Get Attention"
It's unfortunate that this phrase is often uttered in frustration. What we know about children and their behavior is that their behavior has a purpose. Their behavior is communication. There's a need that is being expressed through behavior, even the undesired behavior like arguing, interrupting, and fighting with siblings.

Sometimes, this need is attention.

Rather than addressing this need, parents have been told to ignore the behavior. Sometimes, ignoring seems to "work." The child stops begging, crying, or asking for attention. But if you were to look closer, you may find that the child has simply given up. They may have reached the sad conclusion that their parents do not have the time or ability to notice them or help with big feelings. Some children turn to their peers for attention instead of their parents. Some children get stuck in a cycle of shame. And sometimes, the behavior does not "go away"; instead, it escalates into a full-blown tantrum or ongoing power struggles.

What if, instead of ignoring our child's need for attention, we met the need by giving them attention? What if we prioritized connection over correction?

Giving a child attention is actually meeting their deepest need. In this instance, your child didn't know a better way to communicate their need to feel connected to you. Maybe they needed your help to manage a big feeling or create a plan to make it through a tricky situation. Maybe they were just needing some reassurance that they were not alone. Think back to chapter 11 about connection. Explore ways your child feels most connected to you, and add them to your daily interactions. Prioritize one-on-one time with your child on a consistent basis.

Once their connection needs are met, you can help your child find other ways to ask for attention. You can problem-solve together, creating a plan to use when they're feeling disconnected or when you are distracted. You can help them find ways to ask for attention from siblings or friends. Meeting this need and working together keeps your relationship strong by sending the message "Your needs are important. You deserve attention. I am reliable, capable, and here for you."

*"She's Trying to Push My Buttons"*
Kids have a unique ability to identify the exact triggers that will elicit a response from us. It may seem that they are calculating it all ahead of time, with the intent of making our life miserable. It's hard not to take it personally.

But a more accurate statement would be "My buttons are being pushed."

The question isn't "How do I get my child to stop pushing my buttons?" It's "Why does this behavior or statement bother me so much?" Or, "What feelings is this bringing up for me? Why?" When we look at ourselves first, we're able to separate our children's behavior from our reactions. When we take a deep breath, we're able to get a clear picture with a calm mind rather than responding from an alarm state. The information you get by asking these questions may help you recognize why your child's words bother you and give you a chance to explore what you—and your child—need at this moment. Maybe you'll recognize your child has identified an area where you don't feel confident or where there's something you'd like to work on. (Kids have a way of showing us places we can grow!)

Next, be curious about your child's behavior. Ask yourself what may be driving their behavior? What is your child trying to say, even though they're not using the most appropriate words? What does your child need? Why is this behavior happening right now?

Kids are wired for connection to their caregivers. They are born with the need to be attached—it is a survival instinct! Severing this connection is uncomfortable, scary, and uncertain. While you may think your child's goal is to push you away, chances are good that disconnection is not their goal. On the contrary, when your child pushes your buttons, they are likely feeling disconnected and are longing to feel reconnected.

Instead of pushing your child away when she pushes your buttons, look past the undesired behavior and search for ways to rebuild or strengthen the connection.

As you examine the way you talk about your kids and to your kids, you may start to notice patterns. You may start to recognize that you're placing the blame on your child rather than taking responsibility for your own actions. You may notice you're expecting your children to be more mature or self-regulated than they are capable of at this point in their development.

Changing your perspective may also help you notice the good. Adjusting your "nice-to-nag" ratio can decrease the tension and disconnection in your home. When you take the time to notice and praise your child's positive traits, they may be more likely to display these behaviors. When we adjust our ratio, our kids realize that we're worth listening to. They aren't defensive, worried we're going to say something negative; instead, they're eager to have positive interactions with us. It's not about being permissive; it's about seeing your kids as growing, maturing, and learning rather than expecting perfection.

By the way, how's your own internal "nice-to-nag" ratio? Are you speaking kindly and compassionately yourself? Or are you mostly harsh, negative, critical, or judgmental? Are you making assumptions about yourself or your parenting that are untrue?

Pause and take a deep breath. Change your perspective—recognizing your worth, your desire to move forward, even after setbacks. Forgive yourself for mistakes. Offer yourself grace.

The next chapter will explore the difference a grace-based perspective can make in how you think about discipline.

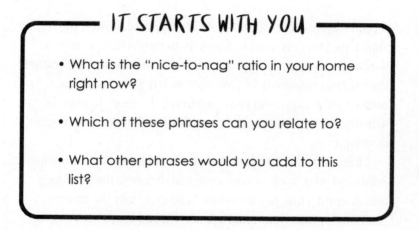

## IT STARTS WITH YOU

- What is the "nice-to-nag" ratio in your home right now?

- Which of these phrases can you relate to?

- What other phrases would you add to this list?

# CHAPTER 23

# Rethinking Traditional Discipline

**The rules of time-out seem fairly** straightforward. Your child acts in a way you see as inappropriate, so you put them on a chair or in their room to think about what they've done.

What they don't say is how difficult it is to keep a child in time-out. Before you can even start the timer, your child is running around, screaming. Avoiding you. Avoiding the time-out area. You find yourself losing your cool, chasing your child around trying to force them into the chair. What seemed like a small infraction a few minutes ago has turned into an all-out brawl. Your child is definitely not sitting calmly, thinking about what they've done.

So you try giving a threat. "Get in here or you won't get screen time later!" Some children will run in, full steam ahead, to avoid missing their screen time. It's not that he's regretful or apologetic for his behavior; it's that screen time is his favorite part of the day, and he will do anything to protect it. Other kids will seem indifferent, leaving you stuck. What are your options now? You can take screen time away for tomorrow, and the next day, but that's going to be miserable for you. (Because, honestly, you rely on that screen time to get some peace and quiet.) You can take something else away, but at some point, you're going to run out of things to take away. And unfortunately, the behavior isn't changing or getting any better.

After time-outs, threats, and taking things away, your discipline options seem limited. You could try grounding your kids from activities. You could lecture. You could go toe-to-toe with your kids in a power struggle to prove your point. You could throw your hands up in defeat, giving up, giving in, or ignoring the problem, hoping things will smooth over on their own eventually.

If you can relate to feeling stuck, you're not alone. Traditional discipline is focused on parent-created consequences that will hopefully encourage a child to behave differently. When we, as parents, run out of consequences to try, we feel like we're out of options altogether.

Thankfully, grace-based parenting looks at discipline differently.

## DISCIPLINE FROM A BRAIN PERSPECTIVE

Traditional discipline focuses on in-the-moment change. We want to see our kids change their behavior in an instant. We expect immediate results. Even if we don't say this out loud, our objective is to find something that will motivate our kids to change their behavior once and for all. Unfortunately, these expectations do not match up with how children grow, learn, and mature.

Self-regulation is a long process. Remember, it takes at least twenty-five years for your child's brain to fully develop. During this time, your child's brain will make many leaps forward in maturity, while still struggling if they are hungry, tired, overstimulated, or feeling disconnected from you. We cannot expect overnight success from a brain that is still in formation.

It's also important to remember that calm brains make good choices. Time-outs, threats, and having things taken away may put your child's brain into fight or flight. When their brain is in alarm mode, they see everything as a threat. Their body reacts to this threat by running away, fighting back, or freezing. You may see your discipline as an attempt to teach or help them make better choices, but if your child's brain interprets your actions as threats, their brain won't get the message.

Our kids are designed for connection. Sending our kids to their room for a time-out or refusing to engage with our kids while they're upset is the opposite of connection. Time-outs send the message "I can only be with you when you are calm and happy." Intentional or not, this message can impact our kids on a deep level. Kids who are susceptible to shame may start to internalize this message, believing there is something about them that is flawed, and therefore unlovable. Kids who are feeling disconnected from their caregivers may push away even harder, resisting punishments and ignoring threats because they are not able to rest and feel secure in their connection.

Finally, traditional discipline puts the focus on children rather than adults. The expectation is that if the children mature and make better choices, the adults wouldn't lose their temper or have to impose a consequence. Rather than looking at how their own actions played a role, how their words impacted a child's behavior, or how their own brain went into fight or flight, immature children are expected to behave better than their caregivers.

We want a discipline that takes self-regulation, brain maturity, calmness, and connection into account. And it needs to start with us.

## WHAT DO I DO INSTEAD?

Instead of working for immediate improvement, we need to shift our perspective, thinking of discipline as a long game. Coming alongside our children as they mature, guiding them through rough patches, and coaching them through mistakes.

The question is, if we avoid timeouts, grounding, taking things away, threats, yelling, reward charts, and point systems, what do we do instead?

Discipline is no longer a five-point list of things to "do." It's not a one-size-fits-all approach that you can apply to every child and every situation always. It may look different, sound different, and feel different.

The answer is—Be.

Be calm.

Be connected.

Be confident.

Be curious.

Be attuned.

Be present.

Be willing to look at your own actions.

Be aware of developmental stages.

Be creative.

Be flexible.

Be a collaborative problem-solver.

Be willing to seek support—for yourself or your child.

It's no longer about doing the "right" thing or following the "rules." Parenting experts Amy and Jeffrey Olrick explain it this way: "'How shall I *be* with this person?' is a two-way-street question. It forces us to look not only at our child but at ourselves, and this opens up a whole new world of possibilities."[1] It's about tuning into yourself first, knowing your triggers, and being aware of your brain's alarm system. When our brain is calm, we can see the situation clearly. We can respond rather than react. We can be curious. We can tailor our responses to our unique children and their unique situations.

Rather than asking, "How long should my child stay in timeout," ask yourself, "Why is my child struggling right now?" Or, "Why is this behavior bothering me so much?" And "How can I best support her in this moment?" Instead of trying to figure out what to take away next, pause and think, "Am I calm enough to have this conversation?" Or "Is my child calm enough to listen right now?" Then, "What is a better way for me to be with him right now?"

At first, your instinct may still tell you to find the "perfect" consequence, there is "something" that you can do in this moment to end this undesired behavior. That's how traditional discipline is set up. But the fact is, sometimes our kids have big feelings that can't be calmed immediately. Sometimes sibling conflict requires your guidance, helping each child communicate their needs and problem-solving together. And sometimes, everyone needs a break, allowing their brains to get out of fight or flight before they can decide what to do next. Your calm, confident presence—your willingness to be—is the most important part. Not finding an immediate resolution to an uncomfortable situation.

This is a very different point of view. And it's OK if it takes time to adjust your thinking and your actions. This can also be a very lonely point of view, especially if you do not have friends or family who understand—or are willing to learn—why this is important to you. While it may seem like a unique parenting position, research is on your side. The hope is, as research progresses, old parenting techniques will fade from our memories and be replaced by grace-based parenting strategies like those discussed in this book.

## WHAT ABOUT BOUNDARIES?

If "being" makes you feel nervous and uncertain, you're not alone. Many parents worry that their kids won't learn right from wrong if we're simply focused on calm and connection. Thankfully, it's not being present *or* teaching; it's both. We're going to be calm, connected teachers for our kids.

Most parents start instilling values at a very early age. We talk about personal space, telling the truth, respecting property, and hundreds of other cultural and familial norms. The messages change as our children grow, but the focus is on raising our little children to be successful, productive, law-abiding adults.

When our kids break these rules, we often feel a sense of panic!

"Oh no, if he hits his sister at home, he's going to hit someone at school. Then he's going to get sent to the principal's office. And if it doesn't stop, he might hit someone when he's older and have even more severe consequences—like jail time!"

Not to mention our feelings of concern for the child who is being hit!

It's normal to worry.

But being panicked isn't going to lead to effective discipline.

Instead, let's emphasize the boundary around safety: "It's OK to be angry. Hitting people in anger is not." We can lovingly hold their hands firmly in ours or offer something acceptable for their hands to hit. We can keep other children safe by moving them to another room or standing in between if it is safe enough to do so. Rather than shaming our children for being separated from others, we can narrate our actions: "You're having big feelings right now and your hands are trying to hit your baby sister. I'm going to move her over here so she can be safe." Or, "I'm going to stand here so you cannot hit each other. I'm going to help you each stay safe."

We can empathize with our children's pain, frustration, discouragement, or disappointment without changing our minds or giving punishments. Saying, "You really want to play video games right now. It's hard when we have to stop playing," sets the boundary. Offering empathy means that you are able to see the situation from their perspective, even if you don't necessarily agree. It tells your child that their experience is valid.

If your child has an extreme emotional reaction, even after you've offered empathy, your brain may switch into an alarm state. The voice inside may be telling you, "Do something! Make it stop!" But we know that calm brains make good parenting decisions. Do what you need to do to get back to calm, turning off the alarm, so you can stay focused on supporting your child in this difficult situation.

Rather than seeing their emotional reaction as justification for a consequence or punishment, step back and be curious: "What was it about this situation that led to him hitting?" Your answer may show you an area where your child needs to grow—"He struggles with losing a game. We can practice good sportsmanship by playing a game together in the evenings." It may help you identify something your child needs to learn—"He struggles to recognize when he's getting mad. I can introduce him to the Zones of Regulation." Or, you may decide to have a problem-solving conversation together: "Let's brainstorm ways you can repair the relationship with your brother." Each of these solutions has the potential to teach your child how to handle the situation differently in the future.

Most children will tell you that hitting others is wrong. Most kids will agree that cheating, lying, and stealing are wrong. Some children will be able to tell you that being rude, disrespectful, or intentionally hurting others' feelings is wrong.

These same children may struggle with self-regulation and have a difficult time keeping their hands to themselves, using kind words, and treating others fairly.

It's not that your child doesn't know right from wrong; it's that sometimes their alarm sounds before their thinking brain kicks in. It may be that their feelings overwhelm their ability to stay calm, and rather than picking the "appropriate" response, they hit, hurt, or act in a way that goes against your family norms.

Traditional discipline looks at these external behaviors and tries to find a consequence to make the behavior stop. Grace-based parenting looks at these behaviors and asks "why" and "how" and "what." We decide that it's more important to practice calming our own brains and wait until our children's brains are calm so they can actually learn and internalize what we're trying to teach.

We can give grace to our kids and ourselves in the process.

If you've used time-outs, threats, bribes, spankings, or other physical punishments in the past, you're not alone. We parent with the information we have at the time. And for most of us, those were the discipline strategies we had to choose from. Thankfully, you are not limited to time-outs and threats to enforce boundaries and limits. In the next chapter, we'll explore options beyond consequences.

You are not stuck! You do not need to continue on this path, using these discipline methods, if they no longer fit the parent you want to be. Take responsibility for your past decisions without beating yourself up or piling on unnecessary guilt or judgment. Show yourself kindness. Acknowledge that you're learning and growing as a parent and with new knowledge comes new actions. This is where progress happens. This is where you can truly begin to feel confident in the parenting decisions you make and the strategies you use, not because they were handed down for generations, but because they allow you to truly "be" with and for your kids.

## IT STARTS WITH YOU

- Which discipline strategies do you rely on most often?

- How can you "be" with your child today?

- Is this type of parenting lonely? Who can you reach out to for support?

## CHAPTER 24

# Parenting without Punishment

**We stand at opposite corners of** the bedroom. Her fists clenched. Eyes glaring. Ready for a fight. She says she's "not ready for bed."

I'm breathing. Trying to stay calm, but I know I'm reaching my limit.

Some parents may think this is the time to give a consequence: "Don't let your kids talk to you like that!" and "Show her who's the boss!"

And I admit, in these moments, there is a little voice in my head that agrees with these statements: "This is unacceptable! Take something away! Ground her! Do something!" I used to parent this way. My alarm blaring. Doing everything I could think of to make her big feelings go away because it was uncomfortable, frustrating, and irritating.

But this is not how I want to parent anymore.

I know my daughter. I know there is more to this behavior than what I can observe. I know giving a consequence isn't going to solve the problem.

So I wait.

It's not easy. It's an internal battle of being present and staying connected and wanting to fight back. Old habits die hard, and when I'm stressed or tired, these old patterns want to come to the surface.

I know waiting is the right decision because a few minutes later, she's crumbled on the floor, crying. I'm finally able to embrace her, so I pull her into my lap and rub her back.

"What's up?" I ask, concerned, not accusing.

The words flow easily. She's extremely verbal, and we've been talking about feelings since she was a toddler. "It's not fair they get to stay up late! I hate being the youngest!" I'm exhausted, but I offer empathy. "It's hard being the youngest, isn't it?" I glance at the clock; it's way past her bedtime and not an ideal time for problem-solving. We'll talk about it more tomorrow. For now, the focus is on reconnection. Slowly helping her calm her brain and body. Supporting her in her big feelings and tucking her into bed.

Grace-based parenting looks different. It may feel different. You may doubt yourself in the process. You may wonder if it's working.

And then, you'll have a moment like this, and it will feel amazing. You didn't lose your cool. You didn't give a consequence you regret. You and your child are on good terms again. It's not perfect, and it's not always going to be this magical, but for this one moment, you can feel confident in your parenting and your relationship with your child.

There isn't a one-size-fits-all parenting solution. You can't take a parenting strategy and apply it to every one of your kids without taking their personalities and temperaments into account. If we think about discipline as teaching, we can see that our relationship plays an important role in helping our kids grow. Rather than being constrained by time-outs and taking things away, we can think outside the box, exploring creative and meaningful ways to help our kids learn to process and express feelings, manage challenging situations, and communicate their needs.

## PROACTIVE STRATEGIES

Since we know calm brains make good choices, we want to make as many decisions as possible when our brains are thinking clearly and out of the alarm mode. Proactive strategies are things we do ahead of time, not in the heat of the moment. These are strategies, interactions, and lessons we can add to our daily routines without having to give them much thought.

Most behavior is predictable. You may struggle to get your child out of bed every morning. Or you may expect a fight every time you ask your child to empty the dishwasher. Your son may struggle with reading homework, or your daughter may struggle to play nicely with the neighbors. Rather than having the same conflict day after day, we can see the predictability from a curious perspective. Looking at the behavior with a nonjudgmental lens tells us where our kids need extra support. Being proactive, planning ahead, and problem-solving together gives us, and our kids, a chance to interrupt negative habits and move forward in a positive way.

Here is a list of ways you can teach and guide your kids in a proactive way. Don't feel pressured to incorporate all of them into your daily life. Pick one or two that apply to your current challenges, and return to the list as needed when new situations arise:

- Practice calming and coping skills. Don't assume your child knows how to calm their brain and body. Practicing different methods when they are calm will make it easier for your child to use them in the heat of the moment.

- Expand their emotional identification and communication. Find a chart with feelings faces and emotion words. Refer to emotions you notice in books, TV shows, and encourage your child to label their feelings in daily life.

- Prioritize one-on-one time with each child independently. Limit your direction and corrections during this time, and focus on enjoying your time together.

- Use miniconnections during the day. Explore ways to connect in a way that truly makes your child feel heard, seen, and loved.

- See the positives. Watch your "nice-to-nag" ratio, working to tip the balance from directions, corrections, and reminders to things your child is doing well.

- Change the environment. Be curious about the way things are set up, organized, sorted, or stored. Is there a simple change that would make this easier for your child to follow directions, stay organized, or keep on track?

- Help your child grow in independence. Even very young children can begin helping with basic life skills. Break tasks down step-by-step; offer a variety of opportunities for them to practice and a lot of grace as they make mistakes along the way.

- Plan for transitions. If you're constantly rushing or feeling pressed for time, make a plan to start earlier. Use timers, calendars, lists, or phone reminders to stay on track. Give your child plenty of time to transition from one activity to the next.

- Think proactively. How can you and your child ease the stress later by doing something now? Making lunches, packing backpacks, and setting out clothes the night before may help the morning routine.

- Create a plan. Most children do well when they know what is expected and what happens next. Talk about the day or week ahead of time. Create a visual schedule or checklist together to stay on track.

- Give two choices. Too many options can be overwhelming. Keep it simple: "Would you like to skip to the bathroom or would you like a piggyback ride?"

- Look for the yes. Instead of responding with "no," see if you can change it to a "yes." "Yes, you can go play after the dishwasher is emptied." Or, "Yes, we can read that book tomorrow, since we ran out of time tonight."

- Model respectful behavior. Your attitude, empathy, and communication matter. Your kids are watching you. Use your influence to model the behavior you would like to see, even if your kids don't display it as often as you'd like.

- Be silly. Many parents underestimate the power of play with their kids of all ages. Singing songs, telling appropriate jokes, or acting out humorous situations can all be a form of connection, encouragement, and teaching.

- Role-play together. Rather than expecting your child to know how to handle difficult social situations or navigate difficult conversations, practice them together ahead of time. Use toys, stuffed animals, or hypothetical people if it eases the discomfort.

- Teach ways to disagree respectfully. Instead of focusing on eliminating back talk, teach your kids how to have a respectful conversation, listening to the other person's perspective, being empathetic, and explaining your point without blame, shame, threats, or ultimatums.

- Combat shame. Watch how you talk to and about your child. Remember, guilt is "I made a mistake" and shame says, "I am a mistake."

- Set boundaries with firm kindness. Limits are important, but they do not need to be handed out with a heavy, authoritarian tone. Instead, use a calm, confident voice, focusing on empathy rather than arguments.

## IN THE HEAT OF THE MOMENT

Of course, no amount of proactive planning will completely avoid conflicts, challenges, and difficult situations. And, despite what you may have heard or what you believe, there is no "perfect" consequence to keep these things from happening. Your child is still learning and growing. They do not have the self-control necessary to make the perfect decision every time. (And honestly, neither do we!) Your child's brain is still in formation, which means their behavior is going to be impacted by things like hunger, overstimulation, and exhaustion. (And honestly, so is ours!) Even the most verbal and articulate children have difficulty expressing their emotions. And even the most intelligent children struggle to manage big feelings well.

Don't judge yourself by your child's behavior. Instead, focus on coming alongside them and giving them your calm support and guidance. Remember, you are helping their brain build new and stronger pathways until this behavior becomes less and less of a concern.

Here is a list of ways you can respond in the moment. You may only use one of these strategies, or you may use two or three at a time. Don't panic if it doesn't seem to "work" in the moment. These are not ways to immediately stop a big feeling; they are ways you can stay present with your kids through their big feelings.

- Calm your own alarm. Chances are, this behavior is going to trigger something in you. Rather than focusing on getting your child to calm down, take some deep breaths of your own.

- Set boundaries with firm kindness. You may need to remind your child of the limits, but keep in mind, their brain may be in the alarm mode and unable to change their behavior to comply.

- Narrate your actions. If you need to set a limit due to safety concerns, explain your motives so the child does not internalize it in a shameful way: "Your feet are kicking your sister, so I'm going to move them away from her so you both stay safe."

- Talk less. This is not the time for lengthy lectures, teaching, logic, or reasoning. Keep your sentences short. Resist the urge to engage in back and forth power struggles.

- Speak quietly. If you're a yeller by nature, see if you can change the volume of your voice. Sometimes, making this change is enough to interrupt the yelling cycle.

- Give empathy. Put yourself in your child's shoes, then put their experience into words. The goal is to help them feel heard and understood.

- Slow things down. Your instinct may say, "I don't have time to slow down!" But getting yourself or your child out of the alarm mode is a priority right now.

- Use play. If your child isn't completely in alarm mode, and they respond well to play, use silliness, joking, singing a song, or other lighthearted ways to connect.

- Give a hug. In some situations, a back rub, holding hands, or another appropriate physical touch can be calming. For other children, their brains may be defensive, even to these kind gestures.

- Reduce stimulation. Talking, lights, music, TV, smells, and physical sensations can all keep the alarm blaring. Do what you can to eliminate or decrease extra sensory input.

- Let things go. Not everything is worth the fight. Sometimes you don't have the energy. Sometimes it's something that can be addressed later. Flexibility is important.

- Refuse to solve the problem. Do not give consequences, take things away, or give a solution in the middle of a difficult situation. Wait until your brain and your child's brain are calm and able to think clearly.

## WHEN THE DUST SETTLES

It's normal to feel a sense of relief when the argument or conflict finally subsides. Many parents don't want to bring it up again, fearing it will fuel another argument. And sometimes, we're just too emotionally drained to give any more energy to the challenging behavior.

There will be times when it is too much. And that's OK.

But whenever possible, circling back and discussing the challenging behavior is key to helping your kids build new skills, expand their emotional vocabulary, explore solutions, and overcome shame. While you cannot rush maturity or self-regulation, you can use these opportunities to support them as they grow in these areas.

Here are some strategies for reconnecting with your kids after a disconnection, argument, or big feeling. As you become more confident in parenting without punishment, you may have other things to add to this list. Use these ideas as a starting point:

- Listen without lecturing. Don't jump immediately into teaching. Your job is to listen well. This will encourage your child to think critically and practice communication skills.

- Ask open-ended questions. Keep your kids talking, learning all you can about their experience, their point of view, or their perspective. Say, "Tell me more ..."

- Be aware of your assumptions. Notice when that voice in your head starts speaking. Ask yourself if the messages align with how you want to parent at this moment.

- Problem-solve together. Review the steps for collaborative problem-solving and start to brainstorm solutions with your child.

- Facilitate problem-solving sessions. Help your kids problem-solve with their siblings or peers by going back and talking about the problem together. Help each child express their thoughts, feelings, and actions, and practice ways to do it differently next time.

- Explore ways to repair and make amends. If someone was hurt by your child's behavior or if a relationship has a new rift, discuss ways your child can make things better. Take responsibility for your actions as well.

- Connect. Think about how your child feels most loved, heard, and seen, and do a few of these things together.

- Return to proactive strategies. Be curious about things you can do ahead of time—or skills you can teach—to make this less of a challenge in the future.

- Seek outside support. If the solution to this challenge is beyond your expertise, if you need more guidance, or if you or your child simply need extra assistance, reach out to a professional. This may be the most important step you need to take right now.

- Nonjudgmentally review your responses and reactions. What can you learn from this conflict? Where were you triggered? What would you like to do differently next time? What worked well? What do you need to continue moving forward in a positive direction?

Discipline is about teaching. It's not a one-time event. It's a way of life. It's how you interact with your child daily. It's how you "be" with them. It's a culmination of modeling, practicing, making mistakes, and learning how to do it differently next time. You do not need to do discipline perfectly to help your children grow up to be successful, respectful adults. Your kids can grow through mistakes, especially if you do the work necessary to repair the relationship afterward.

Through each step of this process, give yourself and your child grace. The final chapter of this book will pull everything you've learned so far together, helping you find your calm, confident center. And as always, allowing imperfection to be a part of parenting well.

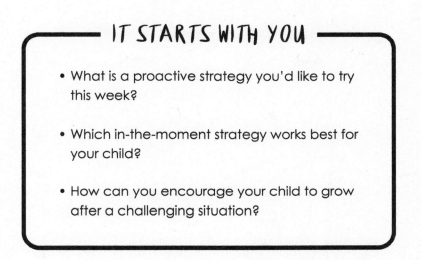

**IT STARTS WITH YOU**

- What is a proactive strategy you'd like to try this week?

- Which in-the-moment strategy works best for your child?

- How can you encourage your child to grow after a challenging situation?

# CHAPTER 25

# Parenting with Confidence

**My three girls have always been** active in the kitchen. I have fond memories of them shredding lettuce when they were toddlers. Cracking eggs as three-year-olds. Flipping pancakes at age six. And making entire meals by age ten.

Each of these stages required a different level of supervision and guidance from me.

At first, my role was to model. To demonstrate how to measure the flour and smooth off the top. I needed to teach them about the hot stove and how to cut safely with a knife.

But eventually, I need to step back and let them experience it for themselves.

Sometimes I stand to the side cringing as they drop butter on the floor or overcook a pot of pasta. Sometimes I intervene, helping them read a recipe or chop through a tough vegetable. And sometimes, I push them to try new things—even though they are a little scary—like putting a pan of muffins into the oven with a potholder.

Just like my role changes in the kitchen, it's my job to change my parenting response to fit the situation. I need to take my child's age, developmental stage, and prior skills into account.

I wish we could apply one parenting strategy to all our children starting at birth and use it until they move out.

Unfortunately, that's not how grace-based parenting works. It's not a step-by-step strategy or even a how-to parent guide. It's about tuning into ourselves and our kids and adjusting accordingly. Every one of us has our own unique history. Our experiences color how we see the world and impact how we are triggered and how we interact with our family members. Our children are also unique. They have their own temperaments, sensory thresholds, learning styles, and triggers.

It requires us to notice and address our own issues as they impact our children. We're no longer putting the burden on our children to "grow up" or "stop being a baby." Instead, we're modeling maturity and seeing our children as growing, learning beings who need our help to manage big feelings well.

If this way of parenting is new to you, you may still feel unsure about what "being" rather than "doing" looks like or sounds like. You may have no idea how to shift from your current parenting to this new way of interacting. That is OK. It's normal to feel some discomfort when you start something new. Let this be a learning process for you and your family!

## TOO MUCH, NOT ENOUGH, JUST RIGHT

Listening, empathy, and collaborative problem-solving are great tools to have in your parenting repertoire, but even the best strategies can leave you stuck if they're not delivered with confidence. Author Vanessa Lapointe says that children need a caregiver who is in charge, someone who can confidently guide them through things that are overwhelming or unsettling.[1] But being "in charge" doesn't mean being overbearing, unkind, angry, or authoritarian. It means being safe and trustworthy.

Sending a clear message that you are capable and will get them through difficult situations, big emotions, and life stressors—no matter what.

When your children trust that you are in charge, they can relax, focusing on growing and learning. They know it is safe and acceptable to make mistakes along the way. When your children are unsure of your confident leadership, they may be more prone to push for control, talk back, caretake your emotions, act aggressively, or struggle with anxiety.

Of course, like everything, finding your confident voice is going to be unique to you. It may take some trial and error to figure out exactly what confidence looks like, feels like, and sounds like for you. It's a bit like Goldilocks and the three bears. Using your intuition, the guidance of a mental health provider, a trusted friend, or a coparent, explore the interactions with your children. Notice when things are "too much" or "not enough" and adjust until they're "just right."

With my kids in the kitchen, my guidance may be "just right" for my oldest kids but "not enough" for my youngest daughter. I may have to adjust the boundaries to fit her, her age, and her personality.

To start, think about your tendencies right now. Of course, there will be outliers—times when you yell when you would normally stay quiet—but for this exercise, focus on what you do most often and in the most stressful situations. Notice without judgment. This exercise is intended not to criticize what you're doing now but to shine a light on areas where you can settle into a more confident posture for your kids.

Do you tend to engage in a battle, or do you tend to retreat when faced with conflict? Do you tend to micromanage every part of your child's day or are you more hands-off? Do you tend to dig in your heels during a power struggle or do you tend to give in easily?

Think about the rules in your house: Are they "too much"? Are they overbearing, controlling, and nitpicky? Are you on your child's case about every little thing during the day? Do you have a list of house rules a mile long? Or, "not enough"? Are boundaries nonexistent? Are you too stressed, distracted, or overwhelmed to set limits for your children? Do your kids have free rein that is more than their age or developmental stage can manage well?

Think about the communication in your home: Is your communication "too much"? Do you tend to yell, argue, engage in power struggles, give solutions, and force your kids to do things your way? Or, is there "not enough" communication in your home? Are you too busy, tired, stressed, or distracted to engage in conversations with your kids? Are you unsure how to have a problem-solving or empathetic conversation with your kids?

Think about the tone of your voice. Is it "too much"— loud, overbearing, critical, sarcastic, or aggressive? Or "not enough"—timid, unsure, or anxious?

Explore the connection you have with your kids. Is it "too much"—you can never be separated; you feel anxious when you're apart; you have difficulty letting them explore or grow in their environment? Or is it "not enough"—you don't spend much time together; you don't enjoy spending time together; you are annoyed or avoidant of your child, especially when they're displaying big feelings.

No matter where you are right now, it is normal and OK. Do not judge yourself during this process; just notice.

Finding "just right" is going to be a combination of practice, learning, and adjusting. It's going to require you to tune into your behavior, triggers, and tendencies and make some tweaks until they fit with the "just right" that is right for you and your child.

It may help to practice different options to help you feel the difference between aggressive, passive, and assertive. For example, an aggressive, "too much" parenting style is going to manifest as tense muscles, an angry face, and may be looking down at the child from above. A passive, "not enough" parenting style may show up as slouched shoulders, an annoyed, uninterested, or avoidant gaze, maybe a sigh or dismissive tone of voice. A confident body posture has shoulders rolled back, head held high, and a kind and assured facial expression. You can try this with your tone of voice as well, trying an aggressive tone, a passive tone, and a kind, calm, and in-control voice. Being aware of the differences may help you make microadjustments in the middle of a conversation or power struggle with your kids.

Confidence comes from within you, but it also requires that you tune into your child. Each child is going to need a different level of "just right" from you. Some children are independent, and they thrive when given the opportunity to try something new or explore a new task. Other children are going to need more support, guidance, and encouragement as they enter a new situation. You may notice that your child does better with clear guidance and reminders to stay on track, while another child resists these directions, seeing them as overbearing rather than helpful.

Remember, we're not going for perfection here. You're going to get this wrong. You're going to be "too much" when your child needs less, and you're going to be "not enough" when your child needs more involvement. That's part of growing and learning. Give yourself grace during this process.

## PUTTING IT ALL TOGETHER

I'm not going to pretend that grace-based parenting is an overnight solution to all your parenting challenges. In fact, it may be the most difficult parenting "strategy" you've ever tried because it requires that you are intentional, tuned in, and willing to make adjustments as needed. It requires that you notice and be curious about yourself and your children. And it requires you to be both confident and flexible, willing to change and grow right alongside your children.

All this hard work is worth it.

You are adjusting your parenting to match your child's age, developmental stage, and brain growth. You're coming alongside them, guiding and coaching them, building stronger brains and a wider emotional vocabulary. You're aware of their challenges and growth areas, and you're committed to supporting them as they learn, mature, and struggle. In other words, you're tailoring your parenting to your specific child. You're not looking for a quick fix; you are focused on making long-term changes.

What an amazing gift.

But sometimes our kids don't see these changes in a positive light. It's normal for kids to be resistant or skeptical of a new way of interacting. They may not trust that this change is going to last and may push against it to test the strength of the boundaries and your reactions. It's OK to name these changes. You may say, "I used to yell a lot in the past, but I didn't like how that affected our relationship. I want to stay calm and listen better. I may not get it right all the time, but I'm working on it." You may have a conversation with your kids about how the household handled conflict in the past versus how you're going to handle it in the future. You may admit that you didn't spend much time together before but that you want to make this a priority now.

Say these things with confidence, even if you're not feeling especially confident yet. You're not looking for pity (or anything) from your kids. This is your decision; it's your role, it's your behavior that is changing. Your kids need to know that you've got this and that they can rest knowing you will be caring for them—even if it looks or sounds different than it did before.

Many of us are parenting without a community for support. Starting a new way of parenting may isolate you from your current community. Parenting is not meant to be an individual activity. We are all created for connection. We need each other to share the emotional and physical burdens of caring for children as they grow.

If you're parenting alone, physically or emotionally, please take the difficult next step to reach out for support. Finding a community will take work, but it is not impossible. There are like-minded parents in your neighborhood, church, school, or workplace. If you can't connect in person, an online community may be one way to find support and have a safe place to reach out for help. You cannot parent well if you are depleted, stressed, overwhelmed, frazzled, or isolated. Your next step may be finding a good mental health therapist for yourself or yourself and your coparent. It may take creativity and outside-of-the-box thinking, but you deserve connection as much as your children do.

Your child may need more support too. As you become curious about your child's behavior, you may notice some things that you do not know how to fix, like learning disabilities, sensory challenges, mental health diagnoses, health concerns, and social conflicts. Creating a team of professionals to support your child and teach them the skills they need to manage or overcome these obstacles may be a wise next step.

But what if this, like every other thing you've tried, doesn't work?

Let's start by redefining our definition of "work." Even with the strategies outlined here, your kids are still going to have big feelings. They are still going to argue with their siblings. They are still going to forget their homework and complain about the dinner you serve. Your child isn't going to magically reach some level of maturity they didn't have before. Self-regulation is still going to be a process. The difference is that rather than being rattled by these normal parts of child development, you're going to see them as opportunities to practice calm, connection, communication, and coaching.

You're going to be aware of your own triggers and decide to calm down before you overreact. You're going to spend one-on-one time with your child regularly, prioritizing your relationship rather than finding the "perfect" consequence. You're going to use brain-building strategies, supporting them as they mature. And you're going to be curious, proactive, and supportive as your child learns better ways to manage big feelings and difficult situations.

But more than anything, you're going to embrace imperfection. You're not going to change your patterns overnight either. You're going to slip back into old habits when you're feeling stressed. You're going to be too tired and overwhelmed to give empathy or connection. You're going to try empathy only to hear your child say, "You don't understand!"

None of this makes you a failure. None of this means this is "not working."

This means you're normal.

You're learning, growing, and maturing right alongside your child.

Remember, it starts with you.

Maybe the most difficult part of this whole process is being willing to offer ourselves grace. To forgive ourselves for our mistakes, past, present, and future. To see ourselves as perfectly imperfect. Important, seen, known, and worthy of love.

If this is the most difficult part for you, it may also be the most valuable.

It may be the thing that makes all this worth it. Because the more you internalize this message, the more you are able to share that message with your kids: "I see you. I value you. Our imperfections make us human. And I love you just the way you are."

What an amazing gift to give your children. What an amazing gift to give yourself.

## — IT STARTS WITH YOU —

- In what ways are you "too much" or "not enough" in your parenting?

- How can you practice your confident tone of voice and body posture today?

- Do you have a community to support you? What are some next steps to take in finding a community?

# Acknowledgments

Thank you, reader. I am honored that you chose to spend time with these words.

Thank you to my editor, Lisa Kloskin, for seeing potential in my book proposal and for holding my hand along the way.

Thank you to my early readers, Lori, April, and Mandy. Your encouragement kept me from giving up and your edits made the book stronger.

Thank you to the teachers, educators, authors, researchers, and colleagues who are dedicated to parenting with respect. Sometimes I feel like I'm swimming upstream; thank you for reminding me that I am not alone.

Thank you to my parents, John and Lynette, for always believing this was possible. Your willingness to learn and grow as parents (and grandparents) is a constant source of inspiration.

Thank you to my husband, Rick, for your unwavering support of my business, this book, and for being my teammate in parenting. And of course, thank you for taking the girls out of the house so I could write without interruptions.

Thank you to my daughters, for allowing me to share your story here. And for keeping me on task by asking, "Are you working on your book, Mom?" You are my favorite.

# Notes

## Chapter 1: Parenting without Shame

1  Brené Brown, *Daring Greatly: How the Courage to Be Vulnerable Transforms the Way We Live, Love, Parent, and Lead* (New York: Avery, 2015), 68–69.

2  Pam Leo, *Connection Parenting: Parenting through Connection Instead of Coercion, through Love Instead of Fear*, 2nd ed. (Deadwood, OR: Wyatt-MacKenzie, 2007), 121.

## Chapter 3: Owning Your Story

1  Aundi Kolber, *Try Softer: A Fresh Approach to Move Us Out of Anxiety, Stress, and Survival Mode—and into a Life of Connection and Joy* (Carol Stream, IL: Tyndale House, 2020), 16.

## Chapter 4: No Robot Parents

1  "Daniel Is Jealous," PBS LearningMedia, *Daniel Tiger's Neighborhood*, 2012, video, 2:02, https://tinyurl.com/2kt9ff4v.

2  Marc Brackett, *Permission to Feel: The Power of Emotional Intelligence to Achieve Well-Being and Success* (New York: Celadon, 2020), 74–75.

3  "Having Mixed Feelings Song," PBS KIDS, *Daniel Tiger's Neighborhood*, accessed May 4, 2021, video, 1:02, https://tinyurl.com/dvfsfhm3.

## Chapter 5: When I Make a Mistake

1  Daniel J. Siegel and Tina Payne Bryson, *No-Drama Discipline: The Whole-Brain Way to Calm the Chaos and Nurture Your Child's Developing Mind* (New York: Bantam, 2016), 220.

2  Harriet Goldhor Lerner, *Why Won't You Apologize? Healing Big Betrayals and Everyday Hurts* (London: Duckworth Overlook, 2018), 40.

## Chapter 9: Waiting for Self-Regulation

1  "Index," Zones of Regulation, accessed February 7, 2021, https://www.zonesofregulation.com/index.html.

## Chapter 10: Completing the Stress Cycle

1  Amelia Nagoski and Emily Nagoski, *Burnout: The Secret to Unlocking the Stress Cycle* (New York: Ballantine, 2019), 4.

## Chapter 11: An Introduction to Connection

1  Brené Brown, *The Gifts of Imperfection: Let Go of Who You Think You're Supposed to Be and Embrace Who You Are* (Center City, MN: Hazelden, 2010), 19.

2  Siegel and Bryson, *No-Drama Discipline*, 42.

## Chapter 14: How to Combat Shame

1  Kristin Neff, *Self-Compassion: Stop Beating Yourself up and Leave Insecurity Behind* (London: Hodder & Stoughton, 2013), 50.

## Chapter 19: Problem-Solving Together

1   Ross W. Greene and J. Stuart Ablon, *Treating Explosive Kids: The Collaborative Problem-Solving Approach* (New York: Guilford, 2006), 57.
2   Greene and Ablon, 59.

## Chapter 20: Troubleshooting Communication

1   Lisa Damour, *Untangled: Guiding Teenage Girls through the Seven Transitions into Adulthood* (London: Atlantic, 2017), 94.

## Chapter 23: Rethinking Traditional Discipline

1   Amy Elizabeth Olrick and Jeffrey Olrick, *The 6 Needs of Every Child: Empowering Parents and Kids through the Science of Connection* (Grand Rapids, MI: Zondervan Thrive, 2020), 19.

## Chapter 25: Parenting with Confidence

1   Vanessa Lapointe, *Discipline without Damage: How to Get Your Kids to Behave without Messing Them Up* (Vancouver: Greystone, 2016), 69.